National Institute for Social Work

Family Support & Prevention:

STUDIES IN LOCAL AREAS

*Purposes and organisation of
preventive work with families*

JANE GIBBONS
with Sally Thorpe and Patricia Wilkinson

London : HMSO

ISBN 0 11 701493 1

Contents

List of Tables

Acknowledgements

Many people from the statutory and voluntary sectors helped in the course of this research. We are very grateful to them all. The researchers' demands may have been particularly burdensome to David Aplin, Jenny Owens, Pat Taylor, David Ward, Linda Wright, and members of the Social Services Area Team in Oldweigh. We thank them accordingly.

Without the generous participation of family members in the two areas the study could not have taken place.

We are grateful to members of the Research Unit at the National Institute for Social Work, and to Professor J. L. Gibbons, Tilda Goldberg, Margaret Harrison, Geoff Poulton, Gillian Pugh, Professor Ian Sinclair, and Professor Peter Willmott, who gave help and advice or commented on part of the manuscript (but are not responsible for its limitations). We thank Professor B. S. Everitt (Research and Data Consultants, Sigma X Ltd).

We thank Sue Moylan, then Department of Health Liaison Officer for the National Institute for Social Work Research Unit, and Janet Lewis, Research Director of the Joseph Rowntree Memorial Trust. The research was funded by the Department of Health and the Joseph Rowntree Memorial Trust.

Introduction

There is not really a clear understanding of where preventive effort should be concentrated or how. ... At the moment there is a certain miasma of vagueness. House of Commons Social Services Committee, (1984), p. 20.

Most social workers and policy makers are convinced of the value of preventive services for families and children. Yet it has not proved easy to demonstrate their success; nor is there a clear consenus on aims or what might be achievable goals. The House of Commons Select Committee, in its influential 1984 Report, recognised the potential importance of a preventive approach to child care but confessed itself unable to identify clearcut benefits from preventive methods. Nevertheless, many local authorities are building up resources in the community which can be used to support families, while residential provision for children in need (as for other priority groups) has continued to decline, and fewer children are entering local authority care. The rate of children in all forms of residential care fell from about 6.0 to about 5.4 per 1,000 of the population under 18 between 1970 and 1985 (Parker, 1988); while the overall rate of admission to local authority care dropped from 3.48 per 1,000 under 18 in 1977 to 2.54 in 1985 (DHSS, 1985a).

It has been argued that residential care fulfils important functions for other parts of the system as well as for individual children. Social workers have been exhorted not to use care as a last resort but as part of a planned programme of intervention (DHSS, 1985b). However, research has demonstrated just how difficult it is to 'plan' what is to happen to children in care, whether they are placed in residential or in foster homes (Berridge & Cleaver, 1987). They are likely to experience many disruptive moves, with damaging effects on the continuity of their education and family and social relationships. This instability may be a function of the system itself, rather than something that could be completely cured by better social work training and practice:

> Our huge, bureaucratic structures make it difficult to provide good enough parenting for the individual child in care. Reading the research, one has the impression of lumbering, elephantine systems that are difficult to handle and slow to respond. When they do respond, they tend to lurch first in one direction and then in the opposite one as management strives to keep on

course. Much of this is not unique to child care but typical of most large organisation. But there are few equivalents to the way in which a system (the social services department) holds such awesome and total power over an individual (the child in care). DHSS, 1985c, p. 20.

The research leads us to wonder whether it is possible to *guarantee* a satisfactory quality of life for children removed into care. How easy is it for the state to match the quality of care provided by even a not very caring natural family, or as is probably the more usual case, a natural family overwhelmed by adversity? If we cannot be sure of providing a better alternative, perhaps we should be devoting increasing efforts to making it easier for vulnerable parents themselves to look after their children well.

The purpose of the research reported in this book was to explore the problems and needs for support of parents bringing up children, and how they used newly-created supportive provision. The book is about voluntary projects and statutory social services offering a personal form of support to children and families under stress. It explores, in two English areas, the demands placed on the social services department area team by children and families in need of supportive services; the availability of voluntary and informal family support resources, how they had developed and how they were used; and whether the existence of voluntary projects made any difference to social work practice with families. In one area voluntary resources were highly developed: in the other area there was less emphasis on community development and the voluntary sector. As the areas were very similar in population structure, the difference in the way family support resources were organised made them particularly suitable for a comparative study.

Diversity of Family Patterns

In the fairly recent past, perhaps until the mid-1960s, the 'norm' and the 'stereotype' of the family coincided:

> Typical Happy Families consisted of a husband-cum-'daddy', who went out to work, a wife-cum-'mummy' who stayed at home, and two children (the offspring of daddy and mummy), all living as one household. P & P Willmott (1982) p. 339.

This typical nuclear family has been transformed by rising divorce rates, increasing preference for cohabitation over marriage, and expectations that married women will continue to work, at least part-time.

Divorce rates have risen substantially for each marriage cohort since world war two, a trend given further impetus by divorce law reform in 1969. One third of marriages will now end in divorce (Rapoport *et al.*,

1982). Rising divorce rates have been matched by high remarriage rates, especially for younger divorced people, but the transition from the married to the divorced state causes considerable hardship for many women and children (Eekelaar & Maclean, 1986). New forms of family life have been emerging, of which the most important are the lone-parent family (often in a temporary stage between one marriage and the next) and the 'reconstituted' one, containing a variety of possible step-relationships. Burgoyne and Clark (1982), for example, identified six possible patterns of step-relationships within the 'reconstituted' family, and pointed out the potential for even greater complexity if the new partners had two or more previous child-producing relationships.

Policies promoting 'family support', therefore, need to take account of the actual diversity in family structure and be adapted to the real needs of differing types of family setting in which children are being brought up.

Family Support: Aims
Social policies concerned with taxation, social security, housing and employment have a major impact on family functioning. However, they are outside the scope of this book, which is concerned with 'personal' supportive services for families caring for children at home. Such services are 'personal' in the sense that there has to be a personal relationship between providers and receivers of the service. Even this restriction leaves a wide range of provision: this book is about a rather narrow band within this range. The reader may try to focus on this narrow band by imagining a continuum along which personal supportive services are arranged: at one end are those with the broadest base—the least selective in their target populations—and at the other are those with the narrowest base—the most selective. All family support services probably share general aims: to relieve stress and promote the welfare of children, for example. But different aims may also be distinguished at different, though overlapping, points along a continuum (Figure 1).

This book is concerned with some of the services, projects or personnel aimed at families considered to be 'in need', rather than with the 'universal' services at the left-hand end of the continuum illustrated in Figure 1. Families themselves, of course, are not arranged along this continuum. Those who are brought in contact with the more selective, narrowly-based services are also making use of universal services, such as health visitors and general practitioners.

Structure of the Book
The book is in three parts. Part 1 considers the development of social work with families and children in their own homes. Part 2 describes contrasting approaches in two social services areas, and how new family

Figure 1
Continuum of Personal Family Support Services

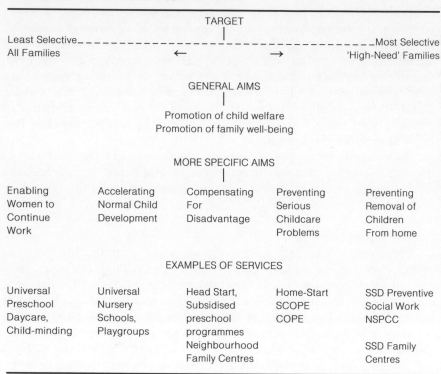

TARGET

Least Selective_____Most Selective
All Families   ←   →   'High-Need' Families

GENERAL AIMS

Promotion of child welfare
Promotion of family well-being

MORE SPECIFIC AIMS

| Enabling Women to Continue Work | Accelerating Normal Child Development | Compensating For Disadvantage | Preventing Serious Childcare Problems | Preventing Removal of Children From home |

EXAMPLES OF SERVICES

| Universal Preschool Daycare, Child-minding | Universal Nursery Schools, Playgroups | Head Start, Subsidised preschool programmes Neighbourhood Family Centres | Home-Start SCOPE COPE | SSD Preventive Social Work NSPCC SSD Family Centres |

support resources were created and managed. Part 3 switches the focus to families themselves, and their own accounts of their problems and sources of support.

Part 1 opens with a brief review of how the legal framework for preventive family social work and family support has developed. It continues with a selective review of recent research into aims and effectiveness. In considering the aims of preventive work, there seemed to be a certain confusion—the 'miasma of vagueness' that also afflicted the House of Commons Select Committee—that made it difficult to achieve a consensus on achievable objectives in this area of social work practice. For this reason the literature review attempts to distinguish between a number of different aims and summarise what can be learned from the literature in relation to each. These aims are: relieving family poverty; compensating for disadvantage or other handicap in early childhood; strengthening or developing supportive resources in communities with many needs; and preventing or reducing serious childrearing problems which could result in the separation of children from their own families.

Part 2 describes the two areas in which the research was set. The development and operation of seven new family projects in one of the areas is described in some detail.

Part 3 describes the research study of three different groups of families with children under 14. Randomly selected families in the local population were compared with families referred to social services departments in the two research areas, in order to find out more about how parents saw their own needs for support and what resources they found useful. Chapter 10 concludes with a discussion of the results of the research and its implications for policy and practice.

PART 1

Ideas of prevention and family support

CHAPTER 1

Family Social Work and the Idea of Prevention

Development of Preventive Services: The Legal Framework

Holman (1986) has pointed out that the idea that the state had some responsibility to assist children in their own homes—to prevent family breakup and consequent removal of children—is relatively recent. In Victorian days the child care pioneers concentrated on providing immediate rescue and removal services. Neither the Poor Law nor the voluntary children's societies had policies which attempted to keep children in their own homes or return them to their natural parents.

Others have viewed the development of preventive objectives within family policy in a less positive light—as a form of 'tutelage', in which sanitary and educative objectives were joined with methods of economic and moral surveillance. Reduction in family autonomy, and in patriarchal power within the family, was facilitated in some European countries by the bringing together of income support, juvenile law, social work and medicine so that, under the theme of prevention, the family became a target for direct intervention by the state—'a missionary field'. Preventive action by state agencies could be justified by families' failure to comply with medical or educational norms.

> In the name of the supposed injury inflicted on its members by (educational or hygienic deficiencies) the family became the object of direct management. Basing itself on the defence of the interests of the weakest (women and children), tutelage made possible a saving and corrective intervention by the state. Donzelot, J. (1980) p. 92.

When the Curtis Committee was set up in England in 1945, against a background of new optimism about the possibility of achieving decent universal social services, as well as revulsion at the existing treatment of children under the Poor Law, its terms of reference precluded it from considering services to children in their own homes. Thus, when the new local authority childrens departments were created in 1948, they had no powers to assist families *before* the event—before the occurrence of specific situations such as those involving children proven to be neglected, beyond control or abandoned.

Handler (1973), in his polemical account of the operation of the 1963 Children and Young Person's Act, described how influential pressure groups started to mobilise at once to repair the omission. The rediscovery of 'the problem family' was a necessary intervening step. A series of studies in the 1950s had suggested that seemingly separate phenomena such as delinquency, child neglect and truancy, were all the result of family failure and pathology. What was needed was an integrated, comprehensive approach which would treat the family as a whole to prevent further deterioration and eventual breakup. Central government was an early convert, accepting the importance of prevention—early help for families at risk—in a joint circular of 1950. This advised the formation of co-ordinating committees, composed of representatives of the main local authority services, to consider the needs of the whole family in cases of child neglect.

There were also economic reasons for the growing interest in prevention. The services provided by the new childrens departments steadily increased in cost, partly as a result of rising numbers of children in care. Packman (1981) described how the first specialist worker for the prevention of receptions into care was appointed as early as 1952 in Oxfordshire. This preventive work, taken up by other local authorities, was much influenced by the Pacifist (by now Family) Service Units and adopted similar methods with 'hard-core problem families' over a long time-span. In 1952 the strength of support that already existed for 'preventive' ideology was illustrated by the decision of the Association of Childrens Officers to embody preventive aims in its constitution.

In the mid-1950s, community work approaches as well as intensive casework were being used by staff in some childrens departments. However, since the law made no provision for preventive family social work, some local authorities undertook none; or did so only when an application for care had been made. Where preventive work was attempted, child care officers experienced

> the frustration of recognising many family situations where cash or help in kind would greatly assist their preventive and rehabilitative efforts yet there were no funds available for them to use.

Departments had to exert pressure on National Assistance Boards, raise money from charity, build up their own supplies

> very much as the voluntary family casework agencies had always done, having few resources beyond social work manpower, but using that manpower to beg, borrow or persuade material goods and money from others on their clients' behalf. Packman (1981) p. 61.

Although by 1956 90 per cent of local authorities had followed the government's advice and established co-ordinating committees (most often under the auspices of Childrens Officers), lack of statutory powers, lack of funds and inter-agency rivalries limited their work. When the Ingelby Committee was set up in 1956 to enquire into services for children and young persons, although its main concern was juvenile delinquency its terms of reference included the consideration of whether the powers and duties of childrens departments should be changed to prevent or forestall the suffering of children through neglect in their own homes. Influential voices were already questioning the distinction between 'neglected' and 'delinquent' children: if both sorts of children were similar products of pathological families, then they had similar needs. 'Preventive' family casework might therefore be expected to combat the rising juvenile delinquency rates as well as family breakup. In its report (1960) the committee blurred the distinction between legally defined neglect and less than optimum child care.

> It is the parents' duty to help their children become effective and law abiding citizens by example and training and by providing a stable and secure family background in which they can develop satisfactorily. Anything which falls short of this can be said to constitute neglect in the widest sense. ... (When parents fall short of this standard) it is the duty of the community to provide through its social and welfare services the advice and support which such parents need to build up their capacity for responsibility and to enable them to fulfill their proper role. Ingleby Report (1960) para. 8.

The committee urged that a general duty be laid upon local authorities to prevent and forestall the suffering of children through neglect in their own homes; and that local authorities should have powers to do preventive casework *and* to provide for material needs that could not otherwise be met. It recommended refinements of existing co-ordinating procedures between the three main local authority departments rather than awarding primacy to one. It emphasised the importance of early detection of family problems, followed by referral to a specialised diagnostic unit which would make full assessments of family needs and refer on for treatment. However, its solutions pleased none of the interests involved, since it awarded primacy to none of them.

In 1963 section 1 of the new Children and Young Persons Act at last gave childrens departments powers to engage in preventive casework and give material assistance:

> It shall be the duty of every local authority to make available such advice, guidance and assistance as may promote the welfare of children by diminishing the need to receive children into or keep them in care ... or to bring children before a juvenile court; and any provisions made by a local authority under this subsection may, if the local authority thinks fit, include provisions for giving assistance in kind or, in exceptional circumstances, in cash.

Packman (1981) demonstrated the immediate growth in referrals and in work with children in their own homes that followed the passing of the act. The whole emphasis, size and structure of the childrens departments changed. This development may have proved even more problematic than the new powers to give material help, which attracted most controversy. Local authorities were now to become engaged with a much wider group of families and children. 'Prevention' was to prove too narrow an objective to encompass the wider range of provision that began to develop in response to demand, especially after the introduction of unified social services departments in the early 1970s. The continuing use of the term, necessary to provide statutory justification for local authority activities, began to lead to confusion.

In the early 1950s, leaders of the child care profession had a coherent set of ideas on the need to prevent reception into care, and the best ways to set about it. They believed, rightly or wrongly, that a minority of disorganised families whose characteristics were described in the large 'problem family' literature were most likely to neglect their children, who would consequently have to be taken into care. In order to prevent this, it made sense to appoint specialist workers who would work 'with' families for many years, providing practical help and emotional support. This approach seems to have become unfashionable, without an alternative one becoming generally accepted. The need was for a better legal framework within which local authorities could provide positive support to families as well as continue to provide more specifically 'preventive' services.

The Children Act

In the interdepartmental Review of Child Care Law (DHSS, 1985b) it was recognised that 'prevention' was an inadequate term to describe the purpose of local authority provision for families with children. There were two main aims of such provision:

> to provide 'family support' to help parents bring up their children; and to seek to prevent admission to care or court proceedings except where this is in the best interests of the child.

The working party recommended that revised legislation should include 'a broad power to provide services to promote the care and upbringing of children within their families' as well as 'the specific preventive duty to seek to diminish the need for children to be received into care or brought before a juvenile court'. This recommendation was followed in the Children Act (Department of Health, 1989a). Part 3 of the Act places a general duty on local authorities to safeguard and promote the welfare of children in their area who are in need and, subject to that duty, to promote the upbringing of such children by their families.

A child is taken to be in need if:
- he is unlikely to achieve or maintain or have the opportunity of achieving or maintaining a reasonable standard of health or development without the provision for him of services by a local authority;

- his health or development is likely to be significantly impaired or further impaired without the provision of him of such services; or

- he is disabled.

Local authorities are required to identify children in need and to make available to them and their families such provision as:

- advice, guidance and counselling;

- occupational, social, cultural or recreational facilities;

- home help including laundry;

- assistance with travel and holidays.

Local authorities are expected to provide family centres within their areas for children in need and their families. They may also give assistance in kind or, in exceptional circumstances, in cash, as under the previous legislation. They are required to provide day care for children in need who are five or under and not in primary school, and they may provide day care for such children who are not in need. They may provide facilities for those caring for children in day care, who include child minders.

Local authorities also have a specific duty to take steps designed to reduce the need for care or supervision orders, and criminal proceedings against children in their areas; and to take reasonable steps to prevent children suffering neglect or physical or sexual abuse.

Every local authority must facilitate the provision by others, in particular voluntary organisations, of any of these supportive services.

The Act provides a clearer legislative framework within which local authorities can carry out their two-fold responsibilities of providing support for families in need, and preventing the need for court proceedings and permanent separation of family members. Local authorities should be able to develop more comprehensive policies for family support provision. However, there will still be a need to be clearer in the future than perhaps has been the case in the past, about what provisions *do* actually promote the welfare of children in need and their families. Local authorities will need means of monitoring and evaluating the implementation of new family support policies.

CHAPTER 2

Family Support: Aims and Effectiveness

There is good reason, on theoretical grounds, for believing that family support, which can be seen as a special type of social support, might have beneficial effects. There is a large literature on the importance of social support in mediating the effects of stress and preventing adverse physical and mental reactions to it. (For recent reviews, see Veiel (1985); Alloway & Bebbington (1987)). Social support (the availability of material, informational and emotional 'supplies' from others) may have a direct influence on individuals' mental and physical health; or it may have a 'buffering' effect against stress, so that those with adequate social support are more able to weather adverse life events. In that case, if family support projects were available to families under stress, they should be more able to cope, and less likely to develop serious and continuing personal problems.

There are a number of useful descriptive accounts of the different kinds of family support projects that have grown up over the last decade or so (Goldberg & Sinclair, 1986; De Ath, 1985; Holman, 1988). Rather than attempt the impossible task of summarising these detailed descriptions, this chapter will focus more narrowly on objectives that preventive services have been expected to meet; and on evidence from research into their effectiveness. The objectives to be considered are: *relieving* family poverty; *compensating* for material or other disadvantage in individual families; *preventing* serious childrearing problems and removal of children from home; and *strengthening* resources for families in local areas with many social needs.

1. Cash and Care

The new powers in the 1963 Act which enabled social workers to give material aid, as well as casework help, to families in difficulties raised a number of difficulties about the purpose of preventive social work. It is not necessary to revive the details of old arguments, but the principles at stake in the controversy are still illuminating. One set of criticisms arose from concerns with civil liberties and equity. Handler (1973) for example, after observing practice in three London childrens departments, concluded that the new provisions enabled coercive state power to be extended over a much wider group of families. The method by which the departments

> recruited and maintained their clientele was through the exercise of discretionary power over goods and services that the clients wanted. Handler (1973) p. 82.

Poor families were forced to turn to social workers for material aid in crisis; but because there was not enough for everyone some rationing device had to be used, and that was compliance. To get material help families had to submit to the casework plan and accept department's control. Social workers assumed that material difficulties were the 'presenting' symptoms of underlying family pathology. Money could be used as a form of bribery to get a family to agree to the social worker's plan. If they refused to accept advice the worker could retaliate by not preventing eviction or by allowing the gas to be cut off. Handler, though, did not dispute the need for social workers to offer discretionary services in kind, as well as brokering and advocacy, to poor families faced with crises. He considered that such practical help should be offered, not as part of a reformatory casework plan, but in the form of specific services, available according to simple eligibility rules, and justified by the mere fact of being supplied to those eligible.

Jordan (1974), who also highlighted the potential threat to civil liberties posed by social workers' new powers, did so from a rather different position. He argued that the 1963 Act was the start of a process whereby obligations for dispensing benefit would be transferred from social security to the personal social services. The result would be to make an unjustified link between poverty (properly the concern of income maintenance agencies) and 'maladjustment' or emotional problems (properly the concern of family caseworkers).

> Casework only becomes an instrument for class oppression when it is used selectively on the poor, as the means of providing a form of highly stigmatised, individualised poor relief, accompanied by rationing devices based on an assumption of the moral inferiority or emotional inadequacy of the applicants. Jordan (1974) p. 119.

Jordan believed that there could and should be a truly universal social services department, available to and equally used by, rich and poor in distress. If referrals were increasingly concerned with 'poor relief', social workers would become swamped with decisions to make on benefits and less able to provide less tangible forms of family service. The subsuming of the childrens departments in the much wider functions of the new social services departments in 1971, blurred their specific preventive functions still further, while increasing the pressures of general demand.

More recent large-scale research into local authorities' use of their financial powers under section 1 of the 1963 Act showed very wide local variations, apparently unrelated to population characteristics. However, the scale of the problem was reported to be quite small.

> Money payments by social workers are quite rare. ... Most payments to individuals are quite small ... essentially occasional payments for special purposes. ... To call this 'income maintenance' is to mislead. Hill & Laing (1979) p. 79.

Hill and Laing showed that about half the recipients of section 1 money were also in receipt of Social Security benefits at about the same time, including single payments for special needs. Most payments from social services departments were small sums for food in an emergency. The link with 'prevention'—of admission to care, of neglect or of juvenile delinquency—was hard to perceive. The picture was rather of poor families, many making full use of Social Security entitlements, but also needing occasional help from another source at times of particular difficulty. It may be that the numbers of poor families seeking, and getting, financial aid from local authorities have risen again in more recent years, associated with harsher social conditions. (Becker & MacPherson, 1986).

Social Services Departments and Social Security
There appears to be an inescapable degree of overlap between the functions of social security and local authority social services departments, contrary to the intentions of the founders of both. The more recent history of relationships between the two agencies has been well reviewed (Stewart & Stewart, 1986). The authors point out that since 1971 the DHSS nationally has tried to promote liaison between its 'cash' and 'care' functions. While recognising that social security had responsibility for meeting financial needs and that local authority social services departments were not general agencies for income maintenance, the DHSS repeatedly drew attention to the minority of 'cases of special difficulty' where both agencies are concerned. (DHSS, 1978; DHSS, 1979).

In 1988, the implementation of the Social Security Act led to radical changes, especially to the system of means-tested benefits.

The problems for social workers attempting 'preventive' family social work arise most acutely in the operation of the Social Fund, which replaced single and urgent needs payments available under the supplementary benefits scheme. Apart from grants for maternity and funeral costs, and to promote community care, all these payments were replaced by loans of two sorts.

Budgeting loans, recoverable from weekly benefit, are available to those with little savings and in receipt of income support (which replaced the former supplementary benefit in 1988). These loans are available for intermittent expenses that may be difficult to budget for. 'Essential' items of furniture, for example, such as beds, chairs, floor covering, no longer attract grants. Money is deducted from weekly benefit to meet needs previously met by lump-sum payments *additional* to weekly benefits. As weekly benefit rates were not increased by an amount which took account of the fact that they are no longer intended to cover only normal day-to-day living requirements, families on income support for long periods are going to experience hardship in replacing or repairing goods.

Crisis loans are available to people without other resources, whether or not on benefit, when confronted with emergencies. These replaced urgent needs payments, but unlike them are recoverable and paid on more restrictive criteria.

There has been fierce controversy over the appropriate role for social workers in relation to the Social Fund, and the early effects of the new arrangements have been monitored by the Social Security Research Consortium (Stewart *et al.*, 1989). Social workers may be expected to meet two kinds of material need in their work with families and children. They may be asked for direct financial help or be expected to act as advocates and advisers on clients' welfare rights. This last role has been given high priority by the body responsible for social work training, which has stated that welfare rights teaching and practice must be a part of qualifying training (CCETSW, 1989). However, while it is true that the majority of families using social services departments are also social security claimants, and that most experience financial stress, it is less obvious that qualified social workers themselves are the best people to act as welfare rights advisers. Alternative approaches will be described in later chapters of this book.

It is clear that social workers' use of assistance in cash or in kind as part of family support provision, has always proved to be problematic. The difficulty is two-fold.

- If material aid is confined to families with serious childrearing problems or whose children are on the verge of care, it may be given as part of a 'casework plan' with all the consequent threats to civil liberties and equity. There is, therefore, a need of open and fair allocation processes and complaints procedures, which are slowly developing.

- On the other hand, if material aid is provided (under simple eligibility rules) for poor families facing a temporary financial crisis for which they cannot get help elsewhere, demand is likely to increase to levels which cannot be met, and social workers may become an unsatisfactory adjunct of the social security system.

These difficulties cannot be resolved without wider changes in social arrangements. Structural changes in British society might reduce the extent of family poverty. Further reform of the social security system could enable it to meet more of the legitimate needs of poor families. Developments in neighbourhood-based advisory services (which need not be staffed by qualified social workers) may enable them to play an increasingly effective advocacy role on behalf of residents in their dealings both with Social Security *and* with social services departments. Finally, changes within social services departments themselves, such as the development of effective complaints procedures, will increase their accountability to their users.

2. 'Compensatory' Family Support: Social Disadvantage

The Head Start programme in the USA provides the best example of a relatively large-scale attempt to compensate for social disadvantage and poverty by supportive programmes aimed at disadvantaged families. Head Start was conceived as part of the war on poverty in the USA.

> Many ... felt that problems of poverty could be solved, or at last reduced, by modest social intervention efforts ... the assumption [was] that pre-school intervention could contribute to the ultimate elimination of poverty by preparing poor children for school. This preparation would enable them to get the most out of schooling, achieve academic excellence, acquire skills, and eventually get good jobs. Zigler & Valentine (1978) p. 478.

The Head Start approach assumed, firstly that environment was the key determinant of intellectual and social development; secondly, that poor children were deprived of experiences enjoyed by their middle-class counterparts; and thirdly, that 'enrichment' of their environment at a critical point in early development would compensate for environmental deficits. Zigler and Valentine (1978) conclude that 15 years of evaluative research failed to buttress these assumptions, and showed that 'enrichment' programmes of the Head Start type could not be considered the antidote to poverty.

The earliest evaluative studies showed that children who participated in the pre-school programmes had immediate gains in IQ and cognitive development. But longer follow-up showed that these immediate gains were not sustained and the whole Head Start programme fell into disfavour. However, later longitudinal studies carried out in the USA under the auspices of the Development Continuity Consortium reported more positive findings (Lazar & Darlington, 1982). Pre-school intervention (in some of the programmes) did appear to have 'sleeper' effects on some indices of later school performance. For example, more children who had experienced pre-school programmes were kept in their original grades (i.e. kept up with more fortunately circumstanced classmates) and significantly fewer were referred for special education. Longer-term gains appeared to depend on the involvement of parents, as well as children, in the programme (Bronfenbrenner, 1974); and on pre-school 'enrichment' being followed through in the ordinary school programme. The emphasis, therefore, changed from pre-school 'enrichment' aimed at the child, where effectiveness was judged by the child's immediate and longer-term cognitive gains, to more broadly based family support with a wider range of outcome goals.

In this country, a large-scale evaluation of the effectiveness of ordinary pre-school provision was carried out as part of the longitudinal study of all children born in one week in 1970. Children who had attended nursery schools or playgroups showed significantly greater achievement on a variety of measures at five and ten years of age. Socially disadvantaged children gained even more than others from their participation (Osborn & Milbank, 1987).

Long-term gains for children and parents

Two of the North American longitudinal studies are of particular interest. In the Perry pre-school programme disadvantaged black children were randomly allocated to a special two-year pre-school programme (which included regular home visits from a teacher as well as attendance at school) or to a control group which received no pre-school help. The experimental group showed an immediated gain in IQ which, however, was lost after the first year in school. However, in subsequent evaluations at age 14, 15 and 19 the experimental group, despite a mean IQ score little different from their average at three before entry to the programme, outscored the controls on some measures of attainment and were more likely to have been retained within the mainstream school course. By age 19 they were less involved in crime; made less use of welfare services; and had a lower incidence of teenage pregnancy. They more often graduated from high school and obtained work (Berrueta-Clement *et al.*, 1984).

The other intervention programme was aimed primarily at parents, rather than children. In the Yale Child Welfare Research Programme, Provence and her colleagues focused on impoverished parents-to-be, living in the inner city and expecting a first child. They reasoned that since such parents face environmental and personal stress and may have few supports, better parenting might only be achieved as an indirect result of services aimed at reducing the adult's needs.

The programme included paediatric care, day care, social work and psychological services, all of which were available to parents in individualised packages from pregnancy to when the child was two and a half. Regular home-visiting was an important part of the programme: professional workers tried to develop a supportive relationship with the parents to help them with childrearing and to link them to other available services. There was also a centre, Childrens House, where parents could go informally. There were only 17 experimental families and 18 controls, matched for sex, income level, number of parents and ethnicity.

Evaluation was carried out at the end of the programme (Rescorla *et al.*, 1982), after five years (Trickett *et al.*, 1982) and after ten years (Seitz *et al.*, 1985). The programme was shown to have a long-term influence on family functioning: more experimental mothers continued with their education after birth of the first child; they had smaller families; more of them were self-supporting and fewer were living with extended families. There were no differences in parenting style or in the childrens' IQ; but experimental children had less absenteeism from school and better school adjustment.

Although the numbers were small, and an experimental design was not used, the positive results are consistent with those from other, more child-centred programmes. The study is particularly valuable for its theoretical emphasis on social support to parents, the ways in which this might be delivered, and criteria that might be used to evaluate outcomes.

3. Compensatory Family Support: Illness and Handicap

Parents bringing up handicapped children carry a heavy burden (Chetwynd, 1985). It has also been suggested that children suffering from chronic illnesses have a heightened risk of developing secondary symptoms of psychosocial maladjustment (Nolan and Pless, 1986). It seems reasonable to think that family support programmes might reduce strain on parents caring for handicapped children by mobilising practical and emotional help; and that this might have a beneficial effect on the children themselves.

Unfortunately, the evidence from recent controlled studies is not very encouraging, at least in the short-term. Support provided by lay family counsellors to families with chronically sick children was shown to confer some (though slight) psychological benefits in a randomised controlled trial in Rochester, New York (Pless and Satterwhite, 1972). A trial of a more comprehensive, professional home-care programme also in the USA, found few psychosocial benefits immediately after the programme but significant gains for home-care children compared with controls after five years (Stein & Jessop, 1986). A randomised controlled trial of social work support in 345 families with children suffering from chronic disorders carried out in Canada found no short-term benefits for the children or their families (Nolan *et al.*, 1987). It may be that the period of intervention (six months) was too short, or the form of intervention insufficiently thought through. It is also possible that longer-term follow-up would show more gains for those who received support.

The results from what is probably the most carefully controlled British study were also largely negative. Glendinning (1986) evaluated the effectiveness of a specially created social work service offered to parents of severely handicapped children who had sought help from the Family Fund. Independent 'resource workers', all specialised and experienced social workers, offered advice, counselling, information and advocacy, over a two-year period, to 107 parents in five different geographic areas. Comparison families, also drawn from the records of the Family Fund, but living in different areas, were not offered any special service. The results showed that although the mothers were very appreciative of the resource workers' help, there were few differences in outcome, on a wide range of measures, between them and the comparison families who had received no special help. In particular, there were no differences in the mothers' morale, and very few in the actual services received. In interpreting these apparently negative results, we perhaps need to take into account that the resource workers were isolated and part-time, without any access to resources themselves and relatively powerless to influence mainstream services. The amount of contact between them and the families was fairly small and widely spaced, and the families were not selected for help at a time when they necessarily most needed it.

Hatch and Hinton's (1986) evaluation of the work of Contact-a-Family (CAF) was rather more positive—though again the authors did not use an experimental design. CAF originated as a voluntary society in Wandsworth in 1974, and by 1985 had about 200 local groups in different areas. It operates through local self-help groups of parents of handicapped children, supported by paid staff. There are usually a range of activities, such as coffee mornings, holiday playschemes and socials. Hatch and Hinton, in an interview survey, compared members and non-members in one area on a number of 'outcome' measures, and found significant differences favouring members on some, though not all, of them. CAF members had more knowledge of available services and resources, which they had more often acquired through other parents; and they made more use of services. However they experienced just as much personal distress and strain as non-members. The results achieved by CAF, a voluntary project giving high priority to developing and supporting *groups* of parents, seem to compare very favourably with the individualised, professional help offered by the resource workers attached to the Family Fund.

4. Prevention of Serious Childrearing Problems

There are few controlled, evaluative studies of the effectiveness of measures intended to prevent serious parenting problems leading to breakup of families. The scarcity in Britain of controlled evaluations of the effectiveness of measures intended to treat child abuse and neglect is particularly striking. Even in the USA, although there is a huge descriptive literature about child abuse, there are fewer controlled studies of the effectiveness of intervention. Azar (1988) has described the many ethical, practical and scientific problems that hinder the development of this type of outcome research.

Treatment of Child Abuse: Findings from Research

In the United States, the passing in 1974 of the Child Abuse and Neglect Treatment Act, which provided federal funds, led to a large, multi-site evaluative research programme. There were four major studies reporting findings in respect of 89 different demonstration projects serving over 3,000 families containing abused or neglected children (Cohn & Daro, 1987). Unfortunately, the research was not well controlled and the outcome measures used were questionable, depending as they did on clinical judgments. However, the large numbers involved did enable comparisons to be made between groups who had received different packages of services.

Two of the studies reported the superiority of certain kinds of package. The inclusion of lay helpers within a treatment programme was linked with success, as was the inclusion of group counselling and practical services. Strategies which relied solely on professional therapy were reportedly less successful. However, the results as a whole suggested that at least a third of the parents continued to maltreat their children while they were in therapy, and over half were believed to be likely to continue to do so after therapy ended.

Rivara (1985) reported on 74 parents who had physically abused their infants and been referred to a Memphis mental health centre where they were supposed to receive psychotherapy and parent effectiveness training. Only about half complied; about a third re-abused their infant—usually soon after referral; and a high proportion of siblings was also abused. Rivara's results, consistent with those from the national programme in the USA, suggest that traditional psychotherapy and effectiveness training are not particularly appropriate as a response to child abuse.

Blythe (1983) discussed 16 evaluative studies of social work child abuse treatment. These were all the published studies that met her criteria for inclusion: they attempted to specify the independent variable (treatment), measure outcome, and define the population receiving treatment. Half these studies were single-case evaluations, of questionable representativeness. Few of the other studies employed control or comparison groups and none used an experimental design. Blythe was unable to draw any conclusions on what kinds of intervention eliminated or reduced child abuse. Another recent review (Barth & Ash, 1986) concluded that available research provided 'minimal guidance' on effective procedures in child abuse prevention programmes outside hospital settings. Although there were more research reports from hospital-based groups, the results were not consistent.

In Britain, the emphasis has been on laying down administrative procedures that are to be used when abuse is suspected and, subsequently, in monitoring families. 'Evaluation' has largely taken place through the mechanism of public enquiries, whose findings have been distilled in DHSS reports and guidelines (DHSS, 1982, 1986). While procedures are clearly necessary to achieve co-ordination among the different personnel involved, the time seems overdue for more attention to be paid to actual prevention work with families.

So far, the most careful evaluations have come from workers using behavioural approaches (Smith, 1984). In a study of physical abuse, Nicol and his colleagues (1988) tested the effectiveness of focused casework, using behavioural methods but within a broader framework of support. Thirty-eight families in which physical abuse had occurred and where there were coercive family conflicts were randomly assigned between focused casework treatment and a child-focused service of play treatment by a clinical psychologist. Families who received the casework intervention showed more improvement in coercive behaviour and displayed more positive behaviour. However, there was a high drop-out rate, and the longer-term effects of the intervention could not be assessed. Nevertheless, the research evidence suggests that behavioural methods carefully aimed at specific problems may have a role in the treatment of physical abuse in selected families.

Controlled research into methods of treating victims (or perpetrators) of child sexual abuse is still in its infancy, but is taking place in a few pioneer centres, such as the Institute of Child Health in London. It may be expected that a cycle of treatment and research evaluation will lead to the development of sophisticated methods of intervention in a few specialist centres. The problem then will be how to open up access for the mass of children and their families in the care of ordinary services.

Some believe that in this field the results of prevention may be better than those for cure. The next section will discuss some of the difficulties in the way of 'targeted' preventive strategies, but there have been some encouraging results from early intervention. Olds *et al.*, (1986) used an experimental method to evaluate an intensive nurse home-visiting service for new mothers-to-be who were teenagers, unmarried or of low socio-economic status. Their results were striking. During pregnancy, the women receiving the special service (compared to the randomly assigned compari-son women) became aware of more community services, attended more antenatal classes, made greater dietary improvements, and strengthened their social networks. There were positive effects on birthweight and gestation period. There were fewer instances of verified child abuse and fewer visits to hospital emergency rooms in the child's first two years. These results, if replicated in this country, would have obvious implications for the organisation of primary health care and especially health visiting in this country.

Prevention of Entry to Care
It has not been possible to identify a body of evaluative research concerned with the prevention of children being taken into long-term care. The large DHSS-ESRC programme of research into care, recently completed, used descriptive methods. The DHSS report on the conclusions that could be drawn from the research programme stated,

> There is no adequate, comprehensive research, practice or value base which would help practitioners to decide when admission to care would be appropriate and for which groups of children. There has been virtually no monitoring of outcomes. ... We urgently need to know more about when and under what conditions aims are more likely to be met by admission to care or by the use of continued preventive services in the community. DHSS 1985c, p. 21.

Packman and colleagues (1986), who studied children considered for care in two local areas, were unable to find significant differences between the behaviour and circumstances of those actually admitted, and those who remained out of care. There were no apparent differences in outcome after six months, except that those admitted experienced more disruptive moves. There was some evidence that preventive resources, such as day care, made admission to care less likely. Packman's research included those admitted under Place of Safety Orders (by police as well as social workers), and this may have obscured differences between *planned* long-term admissions and other cases. As they stand, however, the findings of Packman and her colleagues appear to suggest that, while those considered for care nearly all come from unusually poor and deprived backgrounds, the actual decision to admit does not have a great deal to do with the characteristics of the child or family.

Some local authorities have attempted to find out whether the type of preventive work done by social services departments can keep children out of care. Packman (1968) in an earlier piece of research had suggested that services such as home helps and day care were unlikely to make a significant contribution. Research in Portsmouth found that preventive services grew in parallel with care services and did not substitute for them, largely because the two types of service were used by different types of family. There is also evidence from Scotland that children taken into care had usually been considered for preventive services, but these had proved inappropriate (Reinach, 1981).

5. Strengthening Resources in Local Areas: Primary Prevention

In public health usage, primary prevention has been distinguished from secondary and tertiary. 'Primary prevention' refers to general measures which prevent an illness from developing: for example, by insisting on simple sanitary precautions Indian army doctors were successful in preventing the emergence of cholera among the troops. 'Secondary prevention' involves early diagnosis of cases of an illness in order to intervene at the earliest possible stage in its course to prevent deterioration: for example, screening instruments may be used to detect early cases of carcinoma of the cervix who can then be offered immediate treatment. Parker (1980) applied these ideas to child care services:

> Primary prevention is thought of as comprising those services which provide general support to families and reduce the general levels of poverty, stress, insecurity, ill health and bad housing.

Secondary prevention represents the next stage:

> Once problems have actually arisen help of various kinds may supply a remedy or at least forestall something worse. At this stage services are liable to be restricted to those who are assumed to be at special 'risk' or whose circumstances warrant special priority. Parker (1980), p. 45.

Many have argued that 'secondary prevention' provides an appropriate framework for responding to serious childrearing problems. Under such a policy framework, social workers would be encouraged to direct services at those most 'at risk'; while research would help by developing screening methods to identify potential cases and by evaluating alternative treatments.

However, the evidence suggests that we should be cautious in applying a framework of secondary prevention to child care social work. For instance, Starr (1982) has shown that the use of screening instruments to identify *in advance* parents likely to harm their children must result in the identification of many more false than true positives. Suppose we use a screening test on a hypothetical population of 1,000. The test correctly classifies 75 per cent of the population and only 25 per cent are wrongly classified. If the prevalence of serious abuse were as high as 10 per cent in the population (an unlikely assumption), 75 cases will be correctly picked out and only 25 missed. But to find those 75, the test has also identified 225 false positives—parents who did not abuse their children but were placed in the 'high risk' group—even though 675 were correctly placed in the 'low risk' group. To find 75 actual abusers in advance, 225 parents have been wrongly identified as likely to abuse their children. This problem appears very difficult to overcome when attempting to predict a relatively rare event with no simple cause.

Such high proportion of false positives might not matter if identification and treatment brought only good to those concerned (though unnecessary expenditure of resources would remain a problem). But experience with Intermediate Treatment has shown that 'widening the net' in this way can produce unwanted results. Young people who have been labelled 'at risk' but who then 'fail to respond' to preventive efforts move up the penal tariff and may be more likely to end up in care or custody. In the same way, to label a family 'at risk' for child abuse might cause fairly ordinary behaviour to be misinterpreted and actually increase the risk of removal of a child into care.

For these reasons it has been argued that serious childrearing problems are better approached through a strategy of primary prevention combined with adequate intervention after the event (treatment). There is some reason to think that prediction of *repeated* abuse (for instance) may be more feasible than prediction of whether abuse will ever occur. Johnson & L'Esperance (1984) reported a statistical model that predicted the recurrence of abuse with 74 per cent accuracy using five factors:

• amount of time abused child spends with abusing adult;

• mother figure's parenting;

• mother figure's expectations of child;

• family's use of agency resources;

• presence of more than one child at home.

If such predictive tools were validated then treatment efforts could be concentrated on identified abusers who were most likely to repeat the act. Since abuse will be a less rare event among people who have already abused their children than among the population at large, the problem of false positives will be less considerable.

Primary preventive measures, by definition, are not targeted on individual families identified as 'at risk'. However, they might be targeted on neighbourhoods where there are many sources of stress and few compensating assets. Some researchers have suggested that there are local areas where a combination of social factors produces an environment that is noxious to families (just as infected water from the Broad Street pump spread cholera through a London neighbourhood in the nineteenth century). Relative poverty, high unemployment rates and segregation of families with many needs and few resources into particular neighbourhoods, often with poor housing, will result in a shortage of people in those neighbourhoods who can afford (materially, psychologically and physically) to offer help to others. Such areas in the USA had significant excess of child abuse referrals (Garbarino & Gillam, 1980). In this connection it is interesting to note the apparent geographic clustering of families on a British child abuse register, which was not explained by simple socio-economic characteristics (Cotterill, 1988). It could be argued that primary preventive measures would have more effect if they were concentrated in areas of high stress and low personal and material resources, containing many young families. Supportive provisions would not be aimed primarily at families with identified problems but would be open to all local residents.

Social Work Services and Primary Prevention
Personal support clearly cannot combat general social problems caused by economic conditions; nor substitute for adequate basic social services. But the availability of personal support may make a significant difference to individual families at times of stress. The Association of County Councils (1986) suggested that the need for such personal support is growing, and that an increasing proportion of families is able to survive in the community only because there is some underpinning.

The Barclay Report
The Association of County Councils, in its report on Family Policy already referred to, concluded that social workers needed to switch from a client-centred to a community-centred model of working, as the best way of serving family life. This was the argument of the Seebohm Report (1968) and, more recently, of the Barclay Committee (1982) in its report on the roles and tasks of social workers. The Barclay Report pointed out that the bulk of social care is provided by ordinary people, usually women family members and often at great personal cost. Although 'informal caring networks' do exist they are vulnerable and fragile and it is when they give way that statutory services become involved. To prevent such referrals social work should be directed more towards identifying and strengthening 'natural' sources of help within communities and less to 'the rescue of casualties'. Prevention in this sense would focus on communities rather than on client groups or cases.

Whether this community social work approach does actually prevent recourse to statutory services and strengthen informal caring has attracted less attention than the question of how social workers should be organised to carry it out—the 'patch' argument (Sinclair & Thomas, 1983). This book will not deal directly with the advantages and disadvantages of decentralised social services. It will focus on the provision of locally-based family support by a number of voluntary and statutory groups and agencies. Within a 'pluralistic' framework, a number of differently organised, or relatively unorganised, groups may be involved in building up resources for family support.

Ideally, at policy and management levels statutory services would be undertaking joint planning to avoid operating policies which actually weaken families; identifying areas in need of additional community resources (in consultation with residents and elected representatives); and developing funding policies in liaison with voluntary bodies and local groups. At the level of the area team, fieldworkers would be getting to know the key community groups in their own districts in order to build up mutual support, and possibly trying to assist the formation of new groups and linkages.

There are relatively simple tests of whether such family support policies have been implemented, though evidence of their effectiveness would be harder to gather. An observer might ask for evidence that:

- A range of family support resources has been differentially developed in local areas that show evidence of need (on such indicators as unemployment, poor housing, percentage of children, number of referrals).

- There are procedures for local consultation and involvement if not full local accountability.

- There is a partnership between statutory and voluntary sectors in planning, funding and liaison.

- Fieldworkers in statutory agencies are aware of voluntary and informal local resources and mutual links have developed.

- A high proportion of local people is aware of the local resource network and willing to make use of appropriate parts of it.

- Local resources are used by 'high need' families as well as those with fewer needs.

In this model of family support provision local authorities and other statutory bodies would therefore be engaging in primary prevention indirectly, through their support for independently run voluntary and informal groups. They would remain directly responsible for services to a smaller number of families with identified serious childrearing problems.

Family Centre and Family Support
During the 1980s there has been growing interest in family projects and family centres as means for family support, but they are certainly not entirely new inventions: Family Advice Centres were being set up in the 1960s (Leissner, 1967); and some have even traced the new family centres back to the Victorian settlements (Goldberg & Sinclair, 1986). However, there are features of the contemporary family centre 'movement' which can be seen as

new, in the emphasis on mutual help, user participation and local control. Locally-based family centres might serve as a focus for family support provision in areas with many needs.

Professionally-Based Centres
A distinction must be made between family centres which are part of the array of personal social services delivered by local authorities themselves, and projects and centres which are either outside statutory services altogether, or occupy a boundary position. The Social Services Inspectorate reviewed the 'statutory' types of centre, concluding that their development within local authority social services departments represented an encouraging step towards improvement in the quality of child care and family services (Social Services Inspectorate, 1988). There were broadly two varieties: one consisting of converted nurseries and providing exclusively for the under-fives; the other consisting of re-designated childrens homes. The centres undertook a range of work with referred families, within a framework of good professional practice. That is to say that full assessments were made of each case, clear objectives were agreed, key workers were assigned and expectations and responsibilities were made explicit. From within this essentially 'professional' base, the centres also usually emphasized user/parent participation and the importance of the local neighbourhood to a greater extent than might be usual in local authority practice. Nevertheless, these centres were clearly part of the social services department and had a professional ethos, rather than being a part of the local neighbourhood.

Voluntary Centres
The Church of England Childrens Society played an important part in the early development of family centre provision. Between 1979 and 1983 the Society set up 20 centres in areas which had many factors associated with family stress and reception of children into care. Phelan (1983) has traced this development to a declining use of residential nurseries. Some redundant nurseries became first, day care centres, and then gradually expanded into centres for the whole family, as the Childrens Society became increasingly convinced of the value of neighbourhood-based work. In 1981 the Childrens Society changed its constitution and expanded its powers to work in the community. It was able to found four new 'centenary' family centres, and continued to develop others as part of its regional provision. Other large voluntary childrens charities have followed a similar evolutionary path (Birchall, 1982).

De'Ath (1985) suggested that projects which had grown out of self-help initiatives in the community, such as toy libraries, Gingerbread groups or playgroups, could usefully be seen as 'self-help family centres', since they shared many of the same principles. De'Ath identified 250 centres, using this broader definition.

Common Features

De'Ath found that her 250 centres shared common features:

* Working with parents and children rather than children alone.

* Attempting to relieve stresses caused by housing, income, legal or emotional difficulties.

* Attempting to increase the self-confidence and self-esteem of users, and in many, attempting to improve parenting skills.

* Providing a variety of services and activities for adults and children; and a range of methods of work.

* A commitment to user or parent participation, expressed through a variety of means.

* A local neighbourhood base.

* Links of some kind with a local, regional or national organisation.

Different Models

Other researchers have also identified a number of dimensions along which centres might vary (Phelan, 1983; Willmot & Mayne, 1983). Holman (1988) combined many of these different dimensions into three discrete models.

1. *Client-Focussed*
   * Specialised activities
   * Clients referred by statutory agencies
   * No open-door access
   * Professionalism rather than participation.

2. *Neighbourhood*
   * Broad range of activities
   * Open-door access
   * Neighbourhood identification
   * Local participation
   * Flexible staff roles.

3. *Community Development*
   * Indirect work, staff do not provide services
   * Unwillingness to take referrals or do casework
   * Emphasis on collective action
   * Local management and control.

Hasler (1984) stressed that differences between family centres were inevitable, and that pressure to uniformity might have unwanted and unforeseen consequences. Hasler saw the shape of a particular centre as determined by a complex mix of factors to do with the type of neighbourhood network; the involvement of the centre in formal welfare services; and the way in which it defined and attacked poverty.

Family Centres and Prevention
Holman (1988) in the study of 10 voluntary centres referred to above, found that most were of the Neighbourhood type. He considered that they were particularly active in five forms of preventive activity: preventing the reception of children into care or custody; preventing neglect and abuse; preventing children from experiencing poor parenting; and preventing them from experiencing severe social disadvantages in the home and community. The projects were able to have this impact because:

• They were part of voluntary organisations and so were perceived as less formal and threatening.

• They were open to all local residents.

• They were well known to and well used by their local communities.

• There was a high degree of local participation, in recruiting volunteers and some staff and in committee representation.

• There was a friendly staff style and users were not cast as inadequate clients.

If family projects of the Neighbourhood type had clear preventive aims and were differentially aimed at families identified as 'at risk', their effectiveness could indeed be judged by the extent to which they prevented family problems from deteriorating further, as measured by 'outcomes' like reception into care. However, the Neighbourhood type of centre, as Holman and others have shown, tends to have a different set of values. Such centres are more likely to see themselves as meeting the needs of and open to all local residents. For these reasons, the purpose of the centres might be better described using the positive language of family support. Their effectiveness should not be assessed only, or even mainly, against such criteria as numbers of children received into care, or placed on child protection registers. Different criteria would be more relevant, such as the extent to which they contribute to a neighbourhood's resources, and to bonds between local residents: their contribution to decreasing social isolation among families and increasing social integration. It might also reasonably be expected of them that they should 'divert' families without specialised needs away from becoming formal social services clients.

Conclusions

This chapter has selectively reviewed the literature on possible objectives for the provision of family support services. The objective of relieving poverty in individual families threw into prominence the uneasy fit between the functions of the social security system and those of the personal social services. If personal social services provided financial help only to families with serious problems in bringing up their children, as part of a plan to keep children out of care, there might be some threat to civil liberties and equity. On the other hand, if material aid and advocacy were given, under simple eligibility rules, to poor families facing a temporary financial crisis, demand would overwhelm available resources. The resolution of this dilemma appeared to depend, first, on changes in general social policies towards families (including further reforms of social security) aimed at reducing family poverty; second, on the further development of independent advocacy and advice services; and third, on the development of procedures within social services departments aimed at increasing their openness and accountability to clients.

Large scale research has been undertaken, in the USA and this country, into the results achieved by pre-school services which are intended to compensate for poverty and disadvantage. It is clear that such services are not the antidote to poverty. Yet there was consistent evidence from different studies that early intervention, involving parents as well as young children, does have measurable effects on aspects of behaviour and achievement (though not IQ) many years later. Social services might therefore both help to build up compensatory services and link families in need to them.

As yet, however, there was no very convincing evidence to support the usefulness of family support provision in compensating for chronic illness or handicap in children. It is not yet clear whether specially targeted family support can make much difference to the parents of handicapped children. New and different kinds of provision, involving self-help groups, might achieve better results.

Rather little definite knowledge has come from research about how best to prevent child abuse and neglect; or in what circumstances to offer preventive services at home rather than admission to long-term care. Positive results have been reported from evaluations of intensive home-care provision starting in pregnancy and continuing through the early months of a child's life; of certain kinds of programmes that include volunteers and practical services; and of behavioural treatment focused on specific problems.

Finally, the objective of strengthening resources in local areas with many social needs was discussed. It was suggested that local authorities might operate indirectly, through support for independently-run voluntary and informal groups, and that independent, locally-based family centres might provide a focus for family support activities.

PART 2

THE TWO
RESEARCH AREAS:

Statutory and Voluntary
Family Support Provision

CHAPTER 3

Setting of the Research: The Social Services Area Teams

Choice of the Two Areas

In considering the organisation of supportive services for families with children, it is important to take into account the ways in which local authorities and other providers of statutory services manage their relations with voluntary and informal providers. Many strands of thought seem to have converged in a reassessment of the role of local authorities as direct service providers. In community care, local authorities are on the threshold of a new era, when they will be expected to commission services from a wide variety of providers for different kinds of vulnerable people, rather than provide such services from a more or less monopolistic position themselves (Department of Health, 1989b).

The role of local authority social workers is changing, with more emphasis beginning to be placed on assessment and case management than on casework in the traditional sense. Social work skills in initial assessment, planning, linking vulnerable people to resources, monitoring and evaluating outcomes are necessary for the success of case management. Social workers will need to become expert in putting together individual-ised packages of support, co-ordinating help from different sources and monitoring results with clients and employing authorities. These changes will also influence practice with children and families. Against this back-ground it was decided to undertake research into:

- the demands placed on social workers and the tasks they carried out for children and families referred to them;

- the availability of voluntary and informal family support resources, how they had developed and how they were managed and used;

- the relationship between social services departments and local voluntary family support resources.

It was decided to locate the research in two areas similar in population structure, but with contrasting approaches to service delivery: one area which had at least started along the road towards a pluralistic pattern of family support services would be compared with another more traditional one. Advice from the National Childrens Bureau Under-Fives Unit, (which should not be held responsible for the choice) led us to a district in a southern English county with many voluntary developments of the kind we sought — Newpath. Oldweigh was then chosen since it was very similar demographically but had a different approach to family support provision. Figure 2 illustrates their similarities and differences.

Figure 2
Comparison of Oldweigh and Newpath

	Newpath	Oldweigh
Population (000)	151	116
% Under 16	24	25
% Male Unemployment	10	10
% Council Housing	30	37
Priority to Development of Locally-Based Resources	Higher	Lower

Source of Figures: 1981 Census

The study was deliberately set in two local areas which were demographically similar and did not suffer from overwhelming social problems caused by structural decline. However, the context in which the social services departments were carrying on their work with families differed in the two areas. Oldweigh did not have a systematic policy of developing locally-based family support resources, while Newpath had for some years been implementing policies which gave high priority to the development of family projects in local neighbourhoods. Thus Newpath provided an example of policies that were in harmony with the approach to primary prevention outlined in chapter 2; while Oldweigh had not deliberately adopted such a philosophy and so would serve as a contrasting example.

We were particularly interested in social workers as 'link' or 'resource' persons—intermediaries between families and local resources; and in the ways in which a network of local resources might benefit families under stress. The somewhat different approaches in the two areas might, we hoped, allow us to study developing social work roles: we hoped that workers in Newpath might be playing new roles—since they had access to more locally based, independently operated resources for families—compared to the workers in Oldweight.

The remainder of this chapter will describe the setting of the two areas in more detail.

Oldweigh: Local Population Characteristics

Oldweigh is a mainly urban district in a prosperous southern county (county A). In 1985, it had an estimated population of 119,960, with a higher than average proportion of children. Statistics derived from the 1981 census showed that Oldweigh differed from county A as a whole in having more large families, more overcrowding and more single-parent households. Although its social class composition (measured by occupation of economically-active heads of household) was similar to the county's, it had a higher unemployment rate and fewer households owned their own homes. Only two per cent of the population had been born in the New Commonwealth or Pakistan—no different from the population of county A.* The overall picture, then was of an area sharing to some extent in the general prosperity of the county, but relatively disadvantaged in terms of housing and employment, and containing an unusually large number of children in single-parent households.

County A: Child Care Policies

Compared to its neighbouring county councils, county A had for many years taken a relatively high proportion of children into care. In 1984, however, the county's social services committee adopted a new 'Child Care Strategy' for the future, with the aims of:

- developing community provision for vulnerable families and children to forestall the need for admission of children to care;

- providing family care for children in the council's care;

- using residential care on a time-limited, problem-focussed basis as a means of preparing children for life with their own families, with substitute families or on their own.

These aims were to be achieved through new patterns of service:

Family Support.   This heading covered a range of provision, directly by the department or in partnership with voluntary groups. At the centre of a network of provision in each area would be a Family Resource Centre (FRC). It would have, apart from a manager, two team leaders and six full-time equivalent centre workers, as well as support and teaching staff. They would provide counselling and groupwork for families in difficulties, as well as offering 'recreational and leisure activities' and building up support

---

*All statistics in this section are taken from the following reports of county A's Social Services Department Research Unit:
Referrals, Series B Nos. one & two, 1985.
Research Report 43, Comparison of Areas Using 1981 Census Data.

in the local community. Linked with the FRC would be a 'network of family carers'—current foster parents and new 'befrienders'. The FRCs would have a complementary role to that of area and health based teams. Ultimately, they were intended to reduce the pressure of referrals to area teams by 'stimulating community involvement'.

Residential Care. There would be a reduced number of children's homes, which would become small-scale units offering 'purposive time limited care' for children from their catchment area. The role of residential staff would be expanded, and new training and grading would be introduced.

Thus, if the strategy were fully implemented, there should be in each 'identified locality':

- a Family Resource Centre, offering assessment, treatment and support for children and families; accommodation for a network of support groups; activities for children and young people; a base for individual and family counselling and for neighbourhood work;

- an advice centre;

- domiciliary assistance and community-based workers providing support for carers;

- a children's home with up to 12 beds.

The costs of implementing this strategy were considerable, far exceeding the amount to be released by the planned immediate closure of children's homes, so that at the time this research took place it was not clear whether the full strategy would be implemented. The area team in Oldweigh was aware of the new strategy, but since it promised no immediate benefits for their own work, and threatened a reduction in residential places beyond what many considered desirable, their views of it were mixed.

The Area Team
The social services area team in Oldweigh, with an establishment of 36 full-time equivalent fieldworkers, was divided into four generic sub-teams, each covering a defined geographical sub-area but all based in the same building. The sub-areas were geographically widely dispersed and differed in their social composition. The southern team extended into the coastal holiday and retirement belt and included a larger proportion of elderly people. In the north was a rapidly expanding population of families on newer estates. The two remaining teams covered the older, large council

estate which had a population of over 40,000. The borough's population had roughly trebled in the post-war period, mainly due to the housing policy of the neighbouring city. This city had developed the council estates in the borough to house its own overspill population. Three different local authorities —the county, the city and the borough—were thus involved in the delivery of services and this diffusion of responsibility had always been held to hinder community development. Families living in the borough's council estates were generally perceived as isolated from the support of wider kin networks.

In addition to the generic sub-teams there were also, at the time of the research, specialist staff dealing with intermediate treatment (one worker), fostering (one part-time worker), the under-fives (one worker) and adult placement. Each sub-team could call on help from a family aide. Home help and occupational therapy staff were separately organised but in the same building, with links to the teams.

Intake Work

The area team's referral rate had been approximately 11 per 1,000 population during 1985, about average for the county. In that year there were 5,021 recorded referrals. The area's managers placed a high priority on providing a good quality duty service to deal with referrals efficiently and rapidly. Each day one of the four sub-teams was responsible for duty for the whole area: three workers were normally on duty together in the team room, with the backup of a duty senior. Phone calls were routed straight through to the duty officers who were also dealing with office callers and emergencies that demanded visits. The duty workers filled in standard referral forms about every case and the duty senior checked each form before leaving the office at the end of the day: the senior might often still be checking through a pile of forms at 6.0 pm. Because of the general pressure on the area team a high value was placed on clearing up as many referrals as possible on the same day. The residue of cases would be passed on to the relevant sub-area senior for consideration and possible allocation, or would be left to await the attention of next day's duty team—this last being generally considered bad practice and legitimate grounds for complaint.

In 1985, about a third of all referrals had resulted in allocation to a social worker, according to the county's statistics. The sub-teams differed in their ways of making allocation decisions. In one, the decisions appeared to be taken unilaterally by the team's leader. In the others there were supposed to be weekly meetings where cases for allocation were considered by the whole team and decisions made in the group.

The author visited the duty teams on 25 days over a three month period in 1986, to identify referrals of families with children and to observe the duty workers in action. Some examples drawn from this observation will bring home to the reader the conditions in which the social workers were practising and the demands on them. Observation led to the conclusion that the system was largely fulfilling the aim of providing a rapid response and clear-up service for the mass of daily referrals; that the supervisory system on the whole worked very well in ensuring good decisions were taken; but that the pressure of numbers, the range of problems presented and the limited resources meant that full assessment of a family's needs could usually not be carried out and service was often limited to information-giving.

The main advantage of the area's duty system appeared to the research observer to be the way in which it allowed teamwork. The presence of other workers and the senior allowed for instant consultation and exchange of information and very rapid response, with most duty calls cleared up the same day. However, there also appeared to be some disadvantages, all working against comprehensive assessment and longer-term planning with families.

First, there was the atmosphere in the duty room itself. The duty workers were usually there all day, with other team members coming and going, using the phone, talking or trying to write reports. Sometimes the level of noise and distraction appeared, to the observer, so high as to present concentration and exercise of judgment. At other times duty workers might be sitting with nothing to do, but unable to settle to their own work for fear of interruption, in an atmosphere of lassitude and irritation. All the teams had evolved ways of coping—often by 'silly' jokes and horseplay, sometimes by 'treats' such as cream cakes. Individual duty workers varied in the extent to which they enjoyed the highly-charged atmosphere: none enjoyed the inevitable frustrations imposed by problems with the phone or delays in getting necessary information from records. (Although the area team was linked to the county computer, the terminals were all in the administrative section of the building. Social work staff had no direct access to on-line information and no training in use of the terminals).

The duty workers frequently had to make decisions of the utmost importance over a whole range of clients and age-groups—from an elderly person 'at risk' at home, or a demand for a section under the mental health act, to agitated parents whose child deliberately set fires in the kitchen or a school requesting immediate investigation of possible sexual abuse by a grandfather. Interspersed were trivial requests, some not properly the concern of the department but automatically put through to a duty worker by the switchboard operator. For example, on one particularly busy day, when two workers had been called out to children 'at risk', a call was put through asking for a social worker to take an old person's dog to the vet. The duty worker rang this caller (a neighbour) back, after consulting colleagues and finding the number of a Good Neighbour unit. She was then asked by the senior to fill in a referral form about the incident—since allocation of resources to the area depended on the amount of work recorded. When the senior left, the worker's tension exploded in an outburst about the waste of time involved. This call had cost about half an hour of the worker's time, as well as a disproportionate amount of emotional energy. Many of the referrals imposed stress on the workers, and occasionally some degree of risk. For example, on one observed occasion the duty senior had to tell a worker on duty (in the late afternoon) that she must cancel any dates and go out to confront a family where the child was at risk from the mother's cohabitee. In this case another duty worker had previously visited with a policeman to warn the mother that her child could be removed if her man-friend (who had a history of sexual offences) returned to the household from prison. Apparently, he had now done so. The police were unable to help and so area managers had contacted the mother's former husband. The duty worker was now going to have to accompany this ex-husband to the mother's home in an attempt to remove the child. If this failed a place of safety order would have to be obtained that night. The senior apologised for being unavailable later, due to a dinner engagement. The observer was struck by the fact that, although the cohabitee was thought to be violent, no precautions appeared to be taken for the worker's safety. (The area manager has pointed out that the social worker had previous knowledge of the client and so was able to judge the risk involved. A different approach would probably have been used with a stranger).

Another duty worker returned to the office having failed in an attempt to move a client from a short-stay to a long-stay children's home. Although the client had previously agreed to the move, when the worker arrived the girl was 'fighting mad'. Over the worker's protests, the staff 'manhandled' the girl into her car but she kicked out the window, injuring the worker. The social worker had to return to cope with duty calls—and some complaints from colleagues because she had gone out on her 'own work'—while simultaneously trying to find an alternative placement. Throughout all this her main concern was for her client, who might be placed inappropriately in secure accommodation.

Although relations with other agencies, especially health visitors, appeared excellent on the whole, the demands of other professionals sometimes created unnecessary stress. For example, sometimes other professionals delayed their referrals until the late afternoon and then demanded immediate investigation of a child 'at risk'. This might impose unnecessary late work—as in the case of a headteacher who rang at 4.0pm to refer a case of suspected non-accidental injury he had known about for several hours. The duty worker was very angry since he would have to visit and investigate and let his wife know (again) that he would be late. However, he had betrayed no irritation to the head, since as he explained to the observer, the department's policy was to encourage schools to refer all suspicious cases and he did not want to deter this head. On another occasion a child guidance clinic rang late to request urgent action on a child known to the clinic but where the clinic social worker was not involved. When the duty worker visited the home she found a child with unexplained bruises, some several days old. She and her senior were then faced with a long evening of investigations and decision-making made more difficult by the need to obtain co-operation from other agencies after closing-time (and no doubt by the fact that this happened to be the worker's bridge night). The burden on the duty workers may be seen from the fact that, on average during the research period, there were four new or re-referred cases each day involving families with young children, one of which would be likely to raise concerns about violence, abuse or adequacy of child care. Thus, on most days duty workers had to make difficult child care decisions quickly, as well as coping with equally complex decisions affecting the elderly or handicapped. Sometimes the pressure was extreme: duty teams might have to carry on their work while a physically abused child removed from home waited in the team room with them for hours until a placement could be found. There were no other facilities for children in the building. The calm, reassuring manner of team members in such circumstances was impressive.

In summary, the duty system appeared to operate smoothly and well, fulfilling the management goals of prompt response and disposal and with a flexible but careful supervisory system that generally ensured high-quality decision-making. However, it must have exacted a heavy toll on the energies of the fieldwork teams and perhaps was using up a disproportion-ate amount of social work resources. Many social workers as well as the area managers expressed dissatisfaction with the limitations of the system: several cases were drawn to the observer's attention as needing preventive help which could not be offered. Social workers found it frustrating to limit their response to families in difficulties for fear of rousing hopes that could not be fulfilled.

So long as the area team operated an open-door policy, without an appointment system, and so long as social workers dealt with duty calls without any preliminary screening or diversionary mechanisms, the press-ure of referrals and the consequent limitations on the service that could be offered seemed set to continue. Any change would involve the area team's adopting a more selective approach to requests from the public and developing means of diverting requests that did not require the scarce skills of experienced social workers.

Newpath: Local Population Characteristics
Newpath is also a largely urban district within a prosperous county (B), neighbour to county A. In 1981, it had a population of 150,746, which has continued to grow rapidly. As in Oldweigh, there was a relatively

high proportion of children under 16, large families and lone-parent families. Unemployment affected about 10 per cent of men aged 16 to 64. The proportion of heads of households born in the New Commonwealth or Pakistan (three per cent) was also quite similar to Oldweigh's. Rates of house and car ownership were much the same.

However, while the population structure was similar in the two areas, their history and local organisation were very different. Since the study was set in Newpath because of its distinctive character, the reader needs to understand something of its history and development.

Community Development in Newpath

Newpath was an unremarkable 19th century market town transformed by the arrival of the Great Western Railway works, which inaugurated a period of development that is still continuing for other reasons. The GWR was the dominant force in a town that became

> a thriving industrial centre in sharp contrast, economically, politically and
> socially, to the predominantly rural county within which it was set. Broady
> (1983) p. 7.

When the railway boom declined, large engineering employers opened factories, and growth continued after World War 2, when Newpath was designated as an expansion area (giving it some similarities to the New Towns of the period). Large new council estates were developed for newcomers from the big conurbations. Newpath continued to develop in the 1980s, thanks to council policies which took advantage of the town's favourable geographic position and good transport links to attract new firms, many at the forefront of new technology.

Newpath's history as a 'paternally' managed railway town has been thought to play some part in the strong support for community development shown by its local government. This emphasis on collective endeavour and interdependence distinguishes it from the less planned approach to growth in Oldweigh. As the town expanded in the 1950s, the Borough Council appointed a Social Development Officer to take charge of a staff of neighbourhood workers attached to the new estates. The Council also provided community centres as meeting places for the new arrivals. Harloe (1975) has described how this approach to community development, which focussed on leisure opportunities and represented an essentially paternalistic approach, came to be perceived as old-fashioned, and by the time of the research the Community Development Division of the District Council was one of three divisions within the Economic and Social Development Unit, responsible to the Chief Executive. The aims of the Division have been stated as:

developing conditions for a full social, cultural, working and recreational life for the people of the area ... ensuring as far as possible a fully human quality of community life, with special emphasis on the removal of social deprivation and the encouragement of opportunities for people to develop to their full potential, including of course, their social responsibility and interdependence. Borough Council, 1982.

The Community Development Division was headed by the Social Development Officer. It had a Social Policy Unit and four area fieldwork teams operating in different parts of the district.

The Division carried out its remit using three main strategies: the provision of paid staff to support community initiatives; the extensive provision of community centres and social halls in local areas; and the grant support given to the flourishing voluntary sector in the district.

An independent review of the work of the Division recognised that the local authority was ahead of most others in its commitment to community development (Beazley, 1989). Its effects were found to be manifest in the quality and degree of social infrastructure, the commitment of both officers and members, the comprehensive grant funding and in the vibrancy of the voluntary sector and the huge array of community groups.

More recent changes in local government finance have, however, had adverse consequences for Newpath's policies towards community development.

County B: Child Care Policies

County B had a somewhat lower rate of children in care than County A, and a higher proportion of children in care who were boarded out.

Recognising the special needs of Newpath, the social services department had produced a child care strategy for it, as distinct from the county. In another important difference from Oldweigh, the area team was reorganised in 1981, and a specialised Children and Families team was established. Previously the area had been generically organised, with four sub-offices in different parts of the town. This organisation was felt to be unsuccessful, since the staff in the small offices felt isolated and unable to get access to enough specialist help, such as fostering. The offices were not in the right place to meet the needs of the expanding town, and it was difficult and expensive to recruit support staff. The reorganised, specialist teams moved to central accommodation in the town. Until a redundant school became available, the team had to manage in unsuitable, split-site accommodation.

Policies Towards Family Support

In 1982, the then Assistant Area Director, Children and Families, proposed the establishment of three groups of staff to look at Intermediate Treatment, Fostering, and Preventive Services. The groups were to produce a profile of the services available from both statutory and voluntary sectors, to point to gaps in provision, and to make suggestions for change, improvement or development. The group concerned with Preventive Services identified a number of priorities:

• Establishment of three locally based family centres, in partnership with other statutory and voluntary groups, to which social workers might be outposted.

• Appointment of additional fieldwork staff to allow 15 per cent of social work time to be allocated to initiating, supporting and developing a range of community-based family support schemes.

• Appointment of family aides.

In an interesting account of its philosophy, influenced by the ideas of the Barclay Report, the group stated that the additional preventive resources needed:

> are not just more social workers, although these are needed. ... They are not seen as being used in the traditional, one-to-one casework manner, but as facilitators and organisers working in conjunction with other professionals, voluntary sector agencies or volunteers. ... Rather than appoint specialists to develop some of the innovatory schemes ... it might give fieldworkers more job satisfaction if these could be part of their task. This requires time to be allocated for this purpose and for this to be taken into account in staffing levels. If all field social workers were informed that 15 per cent for example of their time could be spent in a more community work/consultative role and that their caseload would be adjusted to take account of this, it would mean approximately one additional social worker to each team. ... It would require supervisors to assist their staff in caseload management in order to release time for these other activities.

The group believed that this preventive approach would in the longer term mean a reduction in residential staff and financial outlay when less children came into care.

Implementation
The various strategy documents resulted in eventual closure of two childrens homes, and the switch of some resources from residential to community-based services. Over the next four years the fostering section expanded and a special Adolescent Support Project proved itself, though demand was still far outrunning supply of foster placements. The use of Care Orders for criminal offences had steadily declined, due to co-ordinated initiatives undertaken with the probation service and the court.

As planned, three new, locally based family centres had been opened, with social services providing financial help to voluntary sector partners. However, the hoped-for shift of emphasis to preventative work *within* the teams was not able to be carried out in a climate where resources were not increasing, and recruitment of staff was becoming more difficult. Thus, although part of the structure necessary for the implementation of new preventive policies was in place, the social services teams were not in a good position to adapt their own roles to take advantage of it.

Second Policy Review
In 1987, a second Review of Childrens Services was produced. It did not overturn the priorities of the earlier document, but it stressed the need for the department to concentrate on carrying out its mainstream tasks to a high standard as a first priority. Child abuse loomed much larger as an area of concern. The Review noted that 317 Case Conferences were held on abused children in the area in 1986 and that two Child Protection Co-ordinators needed to be appointed in order to chair conferences.

The goals over the next few years were stated as:

- To expand provision for playgroups, nurseries and childminders by providing additional social services staff and additional grant aid to the voluntary sector.

- To provide more 'Acorn Groups' (special day care services for infants failing to thrive and their families) in partnership with the health service.

- To establish an assessment and treatment unit for abused children and their parents, under the wing of Child Guidance. This unit would assist fieldwork staff by offering co-work with families. It would also assist in the decision-making process for termination of access and permanency, by testing and monitoring rehabilitation with natural families as a first step. It could also help in reintroducing children and their parents, as a bridge from foster care.

- To increase the supply of family aides.

Thus the emphasis of the second Review moved away from primary prevention. In reference to the new network of neighbourhood family centres the Review commented:

> There has always been insufficient time within the Children and Families Team to integrate properly and make the most of the preventative resources on offer.

The Review stated that 'having run a barricaded service for many years', due to staff shortages and rising numbers of referrals, there had been a loss of confidence in the success of early intervention and structured preventive work. Although Care Orders following criminal proceedings had decreased sharply, the numbers of younger children coming into care as a result of care proceedings were increasing, reflecting the large increase in child abuse referrals—up from 17 per month in 1983 to 24 per month in 1986, a 40 per cent rise. The numbers on the Child Abuse Register equally showed a sharp rise.

Intake Work

At the time of the research, the Children and Families Team was divided into three geographically-based groups (none of which had local outposts), each with a senior and 8–10 social workers, assistants and family aides. There was a separate Fostering and Adoptions section for the whole area with its own manager, three senior workers (one with the special teenage placement project) and three part-time workers. There was an Intermediate Treatment team, based at the Childrens Resource Centre, with a co-ordinator and three project workers from social services and voluntarily-managed project (STEP) doing preventive work with the 12–18 age-group. There was also a probation-run Intermediate Treatment project. In addition there were three ethnic workers and a senior, funded from Section 11 money, who spent half their time on work with ethnic minorities.

The team was based in temporary accommodation on the ground floor of a large office building in the town centre. All three sub-teams and ethnic workers shared a large, L-shaped room with administrative staff. Because of the conditions of the lease no clients were allowed to set foot in the building. All duty interviews therefore had to be held in the temporary central administrative offices, in portocabins on another site about 10 minutes walk away. During the research period, the team moved to more suitable accommodation in a converted, redundant school conveniently sited in the town centre near the civic offices. It was impossible to carry out observational studies since the team was already experiencing disruption. However, the author was able to spend a day with duty workers and gain an understanding of the system.

There was no intake team as such, and all social workers took part in the duty system. However, there a distinction between assessment workers, who took on new, non-statutory cases for a loose intake period of three months, and longer-term workers. The duty senior received a copy of all referrals for the day and authorised any further action.

The Children and Families team received 2543 referrals in the nine months of January to September, 1986. All referrals involving a person under 17 came to the team unless the prime client was an adult (as in the case of a mentally ill or handicapped adult with children). The sub-teams rotated office duty, with a senior on duty each day. One social worker was on office duty in the morning and another one in the afternoon. A third social worker, in a separate cubicle, took telephone referrals. There was a standby duty social worker in case of emergencies.

Office duty did not take place in the team room, or space, so the atmosphere was less hectic than in Oldweigh, but the duty officers also got less team support. The telephone duty officer, for example, sat alone in a glassed-in space off the main L-shape. He could see and be seen by colleagues but could not communicate except by leaving the space. The worker on duty remarked that he found it quite stressful, especially first thing and last thing when it could be very busy. First thing, the worker had to deal with messages left by the Emergency Duty Team which could involve urgent action. At the same time the phone was usually repeatedly ringing and it was impossible for one person to deal with everything. Schools tended to ring in the late afternoon to report suspected child abuse. Then the duty senior was often busy in meetings or elsewhere and it was difficult to take the necessary decisions quickly.

Office duty appeared less stressful, since there was excellent support from Reception staff who took preliminary details and showed clients into the duty office. During the brief observation period there were three callers, all with financial problems. The duty officer had an up-to-date Welfare Rights Guide and had recently attended a course put on by the Law Centre. He was aware of local advice points—posters advertising their hours were actually on display—but did not refer his callers to them. He felt that it usually worked the other way round, with local volunteers ringing the department for advice, just as he rang the law centre in complicated cases. This duty officer commented that duty work was taking up more and more of their time, at the expense of preventive work which had the least priority. There were increasing difficulties with social security, illustrated by one of the observed telephone cases. A 16-year old had been picked up by the police for soliciting. Social Security refused to pay board and lodging allowance, and so she said she must go on the streets to earn enough for lodgings since she could not return to her father, with whom she was on bad terms. The duty officer had previously provided her with a letter to this effect, but this had not been accepted as sufficient.

At the end of the research period, as conditions in the Children and Families Team became more stable, this duty system was being reviewed and was unlikely to persist in the same form.

In summary, at the time of the research, the Children and Families Team had its own team manager and three geographically-defined (but not locally based) groups, each with a senior and 8–10 social workers, assistants and family aides. There were more resources within the department than there had been in Oldweigh, and plans for further specialist provision.

The Team had responded enthusiastically to the ideas of community social work, in the early 1980s. It had adopted a strategy of primary prevention in the child care field, which was to operate, for young families, largely through a network of independently-run, locally based, family centres to which social workers could be outposted. Social workers were to be encouraged to play more innovatory roles within the community, at the expense of more traditional casework, and this was to be achieved by increasing staff numbers and management support. However, the resources for expansion never became available. If social workers were to spend more time working with community groups this could only have been achieved by their stopping some other activities. This was at a time when the demand for traditional casework was actually increasing, due to an ever-rising number of child abuse referrals. Thus the conditions for a reorientation of the Team's activities towards prevention and work in the community were much less favourable than had been expected.

Summary: The Two Areas

While demographically similar, the two research areas differed in local government structure and policies, and also in the social services department's policies towards family support. In Newpath an unusually high priority was given to community development by the council, and this was reflected in the dynamism of the voluntary sector. Within social services, there was an active commitment to 'pluralistic' ideals which had led to substantial investment in voluntary family support resources. However, although social services had developed policies on how they themselves should change in response to the new pattern of voluntary resources, these had never been implemented. Indeed, there was evidence during the research period of some retreat from the earlier commitment to prevention.

The other important difference between the two research areas was in the internal organisation of the social department. Oldweigh was generically organised, while Newpath had established a specialised team for children and families.

CHAPTER 4

The Voluntary Sector and Family Support

Voluntary Organisations in Oldweigh

In order to 'map' the voluntary organisations and groups based in Oldweigh that were actively engaged in personal family support, information was sought from the Council of Community Services which maintained a list of local associations, from social workers and from families. Ironically, although we had chosen Oldweigh in the belief that it would lack neighbourhood-based family resources, our search uncovered quite a number. The great difference from Newpath was in the lack of a deliberate developmental strategy and mechanisms for co-ordination.

Day Care
Easily the most widely spread source of support for young families were voluntary **playgroups** and **mother and toddler** groups. There were over 70 playgroups and 30 mother and toddler groups in the borough, affiliated to the Pre-schools Playgroup Association. There were about 100 registered **childminders.** There were a number of problems with unregistered private fostering arrangements.

Social services offered support to these groups in a number of ways. Some annual funding was provided by County A's Voluntary Organisations Policy Panel to the Pre-school Playgroups Association (PPA) to support a county-wide network of advisers. The area team itself offered financial support through small start-up grants and through payment of fees for priority children.

The area team supported the development of day care resources through the work of its **Under-Fives Day Care Officer.** She came from the playgroup movement, worked closely with the PPA voluntary visitor, and sat on the local committee, seeing this as an important community development task. The branch was not a strong one, having been established in a relatively deprived area only recently and her regular involvement was helping it move ahead. Playgroup leaders were able to approach her at meetings, and the assurance of support gave the committee more confidence. She gained credibility by her 'total involvement'—'It's not just giving advice as an expert, it's being a member'. She also worked with small groups of committee members to set up new playgroups, of which three had recently been established in high priority areas. A number of problems were encountered which might not have been overcome without her support. For instance, one of the groups was told it must vacate its premises in a school. It was offered two huts in the grounds on condition it raised over £2,000 for conversion. The committee needed support in fundraising. A different sort of problem arose from a church hall. It was offered alternative premises, conditional on its transforming itself into a community playgroup (that is, with a parents' committee and parental involvement, rather than a straightforward fee for service arrangement). The group needed help to develop in this way.

The Under-Fives Officer had a legal duty of inspection. She was supposed to visit each group, unannounced, four times a year to check on staff and facilities and monitor attendance of children receiving help under priority day care arrangements, but could not make so many visits due to lack of resources. Registration of playgroups had to be managed centrally for the same reason. Problems in individual playgroups were fairly common—perhaps three or four a term. The area had only £100 annually with which to support playgroups. With such a tiny budget little practical help could be given, since playgroups not helped might well feel aggrieved. Poor provision was the most common problem, but other issues called for equal tact. For example, a mother managing the group's finances got in a hopeless muddle and the group could no longer meet its costs.

There was a one year foundation course for new leaders, with a variety of eight week and 'doorstep' courses. The Under-Fives Officer made contact with new leaders at the foundation course.

Mother and Toddler Groups. These also had informal parent committee structures. These groups tended to form in response to a particular need at a particular time and might have short lives.

Childminders. All enquiries from prospective minders were passed to the Under-Fives Officer, who then visited to explain legal requirements and the vetting procedures under which enquiries would be made of police, probation, health and social services about all household members and frequent visitors over 16. There were evening seminars for prospective minders several times a year. There were sometimes difficult decisions to take about applicants and she could call on the help of a senior social worker. The Under-Fives Officer was supposed to make regular visits to minders, which was quite impossible, given her workload.

There was no local branch of the National Childminding Association and no time to undertake the community work that would be necessary to enable one to form. The Under-Fives Officer felt minders did not get the support they were entitled to. There was no training programme; and no mutual support. Social services wanted to develop 'sponsored minders', who would be paid a retainer as well as fees to specialise in 'children at risk'. While this might reduce the need for residential care, it was impractical because there were no resources for support or training.

The Under-Fives Officer also acted as an information agency for parents wanting to place children with minders. She tried to give individualised advice, finding out about their circumstances and offering a choice of minder.

Nurseries. There was little nursery provision for the borough (or the county generally). Only one school had a nursery attached to it. There were four private nurseries. A community day nursery had been set up in the borough in 1985, with funding from the government's Under-Fives Initiative. It provided 20 places to a mix of 'priority' children nominated and subsidised by social services, and children of working parents. When government funding ended, the social services department was expected to assume full responsibility and reserve all the places.

Focus 230

This project was not specifically aimed at young families, but was used by some. In the early 1970s the large council estate in Oldweigh had been the site for a three-year action research programme in adult education—the New Communities Project (Fordham *et al.*, 1979). The original aims of the project—to increase participation from the estate in conventional adult education provision—were quickly modified into a much more general involvement of the project researchers with community groups on the estate, and with residents' own perceptions of needs. The winding-up of this programme stimulated great efforts to 'leave something behind'. At this time, the housing department vacated an office building, formerly used for rent collection and favourably sited for access from the estate. A group drawn from the New Communities Project, local officials, politicians and residents engaged in a prolonged struggle to secure this building as a 'cooperative work-base' for community projects. Urban Aid funding for the venture was eventually achieved in 1976.

Ten years later, while we were planning the fieldwork for this research, Focus 230 celebrated its tenth anniversary. It still served as the cooperatively managed base for various local projects. It housed the Citizens Advice Bureau; an Unemployment Advice Service; a luncheon club for the elderly; a Contact Club for people recovering from psychiatric illness (in association with the day hospital); Adult Literacy, Life and Animal Rights groups. The local community policeman provided 'Police Chat'—a weekly informal surgery. Focus 230 was the contact point for Womens Aid and its refuge. Urban Aid funding had ceased, but funding from the county and borough councils continued although with little security for the future. The building was still managed cooperatively by a council made up from the user groups and local interests, and chaired by a volunteer (a retired skilled worker who gave many hours unpaid labour to the building).

Social services employed a full-time, outposted community social worker (Mrs B) based in Focus 230. Now in her fifties, she had lived on the estate for decades, and had been one of the key local people involved in the original New Communities Project. She had served as a councillor and magistrate and was well-known throughout the area. She provided an informal drop-in, one-woman advice service and a link to other sources of help; and supported the volunteers working for Focus 230.

Her methods of work certainly contrasted with the procedures of the area team. Her room, door always left open, was immediately by the open front door. Most of the room was filled by new toys (for the Christmas toy scheme) and bundles of used clothes and furnishings for anyone in need. In the small space left was her desk and a visitor's chair. The radio was permanently on (low). People came in and out with shopping, messages, presents of flowers and visiting dogs, even when an interview was in progress. The author witnessed Mrs B's interview with one caller, who was seeking advocacy with Social Security. Mrs B provided a similar (though perhaps better-informed) service to what the caller might have obtained from the area team: having elicited the caller's story, she rang Social Security and also negotiated with the Electricity Board on the client's behalf. It was Mrs B's approach that was different. She appeared to be on terms of warm personal friendship with both the officials she spoke to—using this relationship to ensure the client's case got immediate consideration. She also 'lectured' the client—on money management, on undesirable additives in crisps given to children and on interest rates—in a way that might have been offensive in a formal social work relationship, but which seemed acceptable to the client in that setting.

Mrs B had close contacts with the area team, valuing monthly supervision from the area manager (who also sat on Focus 230's council) and regularly attending staff meetings. She felt help was 'at the end of a phone' whenever she needed it, and that area team colleagues knew what she was doing and when to refer clients to her. However, she mocked many of the procedures of the area office, which she saw as putting unnecessary distance between worker and client, and she saw her own role as very different—informal, accessible, close to families and non-authoritarian.

Gingerbread

The local branch of this single-parent self-help group had at one time been based in Focus 230. At the time of our interviews the local branch was temporarily in abeyance. The former organisers had remarried and nobody had as yet taken over. We were told that ups and downs of this sort characterised the Gingerbread branch.

Off The Record

This voluntary organisation for young people had been established in 1977, through the efforts of workers in local probation, youth and community and social services, as well as concerned residents. Off The Record's objective is to 'relieve and prevent suffering caused by mental or physical ill health or by social or economic circumstances among the young people of the borough and the surrounding area'. Its base was the centrally sited Methodist church. After a difficult start, and the departure of the first co-ordinator, OTR had developed strongly. By 1987 it had over 40 voluntary counsellors, all of whom had taken a 13 week training course organised by OTR itself. They were supported by a team of eight people, employed under the (then) Community Programme, who were particularly concerned with finding accommodation for young people and supporting landladies/lords. This team had produced an excellent 'Leaving Home' booklet, which was widely distributed through sessions at schools. The counsellors provided a five-day-week service, as well as three evening sessions, and dealt with some 200 enquiries a month.

Off The Record had one full-time paid co-ordinator. Its management committee included OTR representatives and representatives from probation, social services and education. Representatives of other local voluntary and statutory groups were invited to general meetings. The current chair was from the social services area team, and OTR had developed a joint project with another area team to help young people leaving care. The co-ordinator felt that good relationships with statutory bodies were critical to success. The relationships were cooperative, but Off The Record was able to retain its independence and determine its own policy.

Funding came from the county and borough councils; from fund-raising by volunteers; and from donations from local firms. The co-ordinator regretted that sources of funding were not more stable. Most of her time had to be devoted to fund-raising, and this meant that developmental work had to take second place. However, Off The Record appeared a striking illustration of successful partnership between statutory organisations and voluntary effort. Success had brought about expansion and a new branch was about to open in a neighbouring city.

Parent Helpline

We learned that a confidential telephone counselling service run by volunteers existed on the same premises as the community day nursery. This was aimed at parents under stress, who feared they might harm their children. However, several phone calls failed to gain a reply and we are unable to include further information on the Helpline.

Home-Start

Home-Start, a voluntary home visiting scheme offering support, friendship and practical help to families with children under five, was started by Margaret Harrison in Leicester in 1973. By 1986 there were some 50 branches in different parts of the country, supported by the Home-Start Consultancy. Home-Start works through trained volunteers, supported by a paid organiser who is responsible to a local management committee. The volunteers are all parents: no other qualification is demanded, but all have to complete a training programme organised by Home-Start. The organiser recruits the volunteers, organises training, matches trained volunteers to families, and supports them thereafter. Families are referred, mainly by social services and health visitors, and the organiser visits each new referral. Evaluative studies of Home-Start have been published (Van der Eyken, 1982; Gibbons & Thorpe, 1989).

The branch in Oldweigh was formed in 1983, after two county councillors had been impressed by hearing Margaret Harrison speak at a conference. As always happens when a new Home-Start branch is to be set up, strong local support had to be demonstrated by the creation of a local steering committee, drawn from statutory and voluntary bodies. Funding was obtained from the county's social services committee for the appointment of an organiser and a secretary. The office was established in small premises in the grounds of a convent—not very convenient of access. The social services area manager was closely involved in the formation of the branch and continued to serve on its management committee. In its first 20 months, Home-Start recruited 35 volunteers, most of whom were matched to referred families. It opened a toy library and a drop-in centre, open twice a month. The very success of the branch led to increasing pressure on the organiser. By 1986, 55 families were being visited. The annual report commented:

> Almost half of the families with whom we are working require more than befriending and many of our volunteers become involved with the families' complex problems. This increases pressure on our service and means volunteers tend to be needed by the family for much longer periods than was first envisaged.

Some members of the local branch expressed concern that pressure on statutory services meant that professional workers were less and less able to provide personal help to families, even when there were difficult problems. This might mean that Home-Start volunteers were taking on tasks which more properly belonged to statutory working.

Voluntary Family Support Resources in Newpath

Newpath had even less **day nursery** provision than Oldweigh, though the Education Department was providing substantially more **nursery classes.** The main provision of day care was through playgroups and childminders, as in Oldweigh. The social services **Under-Fives Day Care Officer** had a similar role in Newpath, and was equally short of time and resources. Newpath had a great wealth of voluntary provision, much of which had some relevance to families. This chapter will focus on seven new projects, established since 1981, which were intended to benefit families with young children. Five of these were locally based family projects set up as part of a deliberate strategy.

This section will describe how the seven projects came to be established. The information was drawn from analysis of policy documents that have survived—original grant applications and policy statements—and tape-recorded interviews (conducted by Sally Thorpe) with project leaders and representatives from funding agencies. The projects are listed in Table 4i.

Table 4i
The Family Projects

Project	Year	Principal Original Funders	Neighbourhood Base	Budget 1988
Herding	1981	Childrens Society + County Council	Yes	29,000
Home-Start	1982	Health (Joint Finance)	No	37,380
Newton	1983	National Childrens Home + County Council	Yes	52,000
Hilldon	1983	Urban Aid	Yes	21,000
Acorn	1984	Childrens Society + Health (Joint Finance)	Yes	40,000
Ashgrove	1985	Urban Aid	Yes	54,000
Meadow	1988	NSPCC + County Council	Yes	NK

In the early 1970s, family support provision for young families in Newpath consisted only of private playgroups and nurseries. Then in 1974 a group of women got together, with the support of the commission for Racial Equality and the Pre-School Playgroups Association, to found a voluntary nursery with premises in a Church hall—the Newpath Family Centre. This was achieved with little help from statutory social services. However, an alliance then formed between the Area Officer of the Social Services Department, the council's Social Development Officer and (later) the Co-ordinator of the Voluntary Services Council. This powerful local grouping became convinced of the need for locally based provision for young families, in the form of family centres. The Joint Advisory Committee for Under-Fives shared this view. At this stage, those involved had rather different purposes. For some, the need was seen mainly as the provision of day care for under-fives, and a local referral point for residents to have easy access to professional workers from different agencies. However, there was also an expectation that workers in the centres would promote community groups, advocate on behalf of community members, and prevent the need for referral to statutory agencies.

The First Family Project: Herding
The key local figures were strongly committed to concepts of 'pluralism' and 'partnership' between statutory and voluntary sectors in the development of welfare. It was also clear that ambitious plans for a network of locally based family support centres would be difficult to fund locally. Thus for a mixture of ideological and practical reasons, it was decided to draw in the national voluntary childrens charities. The Social Development Officer put up to the Childrens Society an idea for a new development in the community to coincide with the Society's centenary. The council's Community Development Division undertook a survey which demonstrated the need for more provision on the Herding estate, as it ranked high on indicators of social malaise such as juvenile court appearances, social services referrals and supplementary benefits recipients. At the same time, the Education Department were convinced of the need for a nursery school in the area. A joint working party with representatives from Social Services, Education, Community Development and the Childrens Society was formed and in 1978 put forward a proposal for the new project, whose broad aim was 'to prevent and alleviate stress in families and to respond to the needs of the area'. The project, which opened in 1981, consisted of three Childrens Society workers, one of whom was the project leader; nursery staff funded by the Education Department; and clerical support funded by Social Services. The project was based in a hut next to the primary school.

   Administrative responsibility was split between the Education Department (the nursery) and the Childrens Society (the Centre). Detailed objectives for the Centre were first formulated by the newly appointed Project Leader, with her support group drawn from the constituent agencies. A broad approach to preventive work was justified in the following terms:

• if prevention is about preventing problems that have not occurred then everyone is potentially vulnerable;

• if the area is to change its image and be viewed in a more positive way we must not further stigmatise it by working only with those who have problems;

• if we are to develop the resources of the area then we will need to identify and work closely with the most active members of the community;

- if we wish to foster networks of support then we want these to contain a mixture and balance of people with different strengths, problems, etc.

The Herding Centre's approach was summarised as being:

Accessible—physically by being in the centre of a small estate, psychologically because it was for everyone, not just those with problems. There should be no stigma attached to being seen there.

Informal—minimal bureaucracy and hierarchy.

Reciprocal—blurring boundaries between helpers and helped.

Work on developing the Centre's objectives, and attempting to relate its activities to its stated objectives, went on throughout its first few years, a time of very active team building (Adams et al., 1983). The fact that the team consisted of individuals of different status and responsible to different employers with different conditions of employment contributed to the difficulty in clarifying objectives. There were differences in objectives held by nursery staff—whose first priority was to deliver good quality day care—and other project workers who were more concerned with enabling local users to run their own affairs and activities: they were less concerned with service delivery and more concerned with facilitating the development of self-running groups.

The way in which specific activities developed seems to have had a great deal to do with the wishes and the energy of local people. For example, one of the first activities—Keep Fit—was started because one or two women mentioned an interest in it, were asked to find out how many others would be interested, and recruited a group. This first requested activity was seen by the Project Leader as having an important influence on the Centre's development:

The fact that the class materialised at all must have communicated the fact that if people really wanted something to happen they were more likely to bring it about if they found others with similar ideas.

From the Keep Fit class evolved several other activities, largely organised by users, such as Centre outings, jumble sales to subsidise costs, an Open Day, and a Toy Library. The Family Link home visiting scheme also started up from an initiative of three of the original Keep Fit enthusiasts. This kind of development illustrates how distinctions between helpers and helped became blurred. There was not a class of 'helpers' separated from 'clients'. The same person could be receiving help, say with a financial problem, and playing a leadership role by helping to initiate and run activities. In the same way, a person who originally came along to a family project simply to make use of one facility there (like Keep Fit) might develop a deeper involvement, taking on new responsibilities.

After the first two years, an evaluation of users' views of the Centre was carried out by a Childrens Society researcher (Adams *et al.*, 1983). Three hundred and thirty-two 'user households' on the estate were identified, and three subsamples were selected for intensive interview. These represented heavy users—who had taken part in five or more activities (10); users of the nursery (10); and playscheme users (10). A census of all users in one week was also made; and a sample of non-users (neighbours of the interview subsamples) was interviewed. There were a number of difficulties in carrying out interviews, but eventually 26 users and 22 non-users were seen.

The author concluded that the Centre was reaching a significant proportion of the disadvantaged members of the community, and that over three-quarters of the users had children under five. Although there was thankfulness for the existence of the nursery, there were a number of differences between nursery staff and parents and partnership between the two sides had not been achieved. There was evidence that the Centre was not as well known in the local community as might be desired, and that it tended to be perceived as a resource for people with problems, not a resource for the whole local population. A large minority of users came from beyond the immediate catchment area. There were many 'marginal users', who appeared to have had needs but not to have been drawn in. There was a perceived lack of clarity as to where the roles of professional and volunteer began and ended, and as to the Centre's power structure.

This small research project succeeded in identifying important issues, which apply to the family projects in general.

The Newton Family Project
With the successful establishment of the Herding Centre, the Social Services Area Officer and the Social Development Office turned their attention to fund-raising for additional family projects. They negotiated with the National Childrens Home (NCH) who eventually agreed to put in funding themselves for a family centre on a development area of Newpath. This expansion area was expected to accommodate 25,000 'incomers' by 1986, most of whom would be young families or couples preparing to have children. The development was planned around three urban 'villages', each with its own school, church, pub and community centre with a new town centre with major facilities. Houses were built for sale as well as for rent by the local authority, private builders and a housing association. The area was fairly well supplied with playgroups. Altogether, it faced different problems from Herding.

The new project began in 1983 in one room rented from the council. Its aims were described as follows:

The dynamics of any newly-formed community are predictable along very general lines. It can be assumed that many families manage their affairs well without any specific help, using community resources to best advantage. Others just manage to scrape by, only avoiding crises—debts, depression, rent arrears, unemployment—by a small margin, while a few can become overwhelmed and unable to cope. From time to time stress engulfs a family irrespective of social group and if ready help is not available from neighbourhood social networks the family can slip rapidly from being self-sufficient to a state of dependence on the statutory services.

The new expansion area was expected to cause stress in some families, since they would become new parents without extended family support; the cost of housing was high; there was a lack of day care facilities which would make it difficult for mothers to work; and the numbers of 'latch-key' children would increase as more families needed two incomes to meet expenses. In very general terms, the aim of the Project was to assess the primary needs and then build up self-help and other voluntary groups of people from the community in order to encourage neighbourhood care and support.

There was one project worker employed by the National Childrens Home and a part-time clerical worker. The first steps were to publicise the Project's existence and to set up a programme under which volunteers were recruited and trained. Befrienders were attached to families experiencing periods of difficulty. A day-fostering service was initiated. The Law Centre provided training in welfare rights advice, and subsequent backup, and evening advice points were set up in local areas. However this arrangement could not be sustained.

It was then decided to expand the work of the Project into a new building, which would provide a focus for activities and groupwork. A new professionally qualified senior project worker was appointed in 1985. The NCH bought an ordinary house on one of the 'villages' which became the new base. In the transitional period, activities had dwindled, so that the Project was to some extent making a new start in 1985. In particular, the day-fostering service was ended, and the emphasis on self-help, as opposed to service-delivery, was strengthened.

Ashgrove Neighbourhood Centre
The history of this project is a complicated one. As we have already seen, the Newpath Family Centre, which started in 1976 as a day nursery for working parents, with after-school and holiday care schemes, had pioneered the development of family projects in Newpath. However, it did not have a local neighbourhood base. There was some doubt over the direction in which the Centre should develop, and this led to the involvement of another national voluntary body—Save the Children (SCF). SCF agreed to

provide limited funding for a project worker, who carried out some research and produced a report which led to a clarification of the Centre's new role and an acceptance of a local, instead of a town-wide base. In 1982 the Centre moved to Ashgrove, an estate identified as having many social needs.

The Ashgrove Centre received funding from the County Council, from parental fees, and from time-limited grants from Save the Children and the Hambro Charitable Trust. In 1982, its activities fell into two groups: those centred around day care and out-of-school and holiday schemes; and a limited amount of neighbourhood work with parents. The Centre was staffed by a Project Leader, a Nursery Supervisor and nursery staff.

In 1984–5, the Centre experienced major change. As with the other projects, the emphasis shifted from providing day care to a more loosely defined 'family support'. The nursery continued, but in a new guise, as part of Education Department provision. The Ashgrove Neighbourhood Centre was reconstituted, in order to:

- alleviate the effects of social stress and disadvantage experienced by families and/or individuals living within the area;

- where necessary to assist families and/or individuals to meet their diverse social, educational, cultural, health and welfare needs;

- provide, promote and contribute to the establishment of such facilities and activities as are required by families and/or individuals, such as premises for meetings, counselling and support, information and advice.

The newly constituted project was funded through an Urban Aid grant.

Hilldon Neighbourhood Centre

Hilldon consists mainly of council dwellings built in the 1950s, with three high-rise blocks built in the 1960s. It is an area of high unemployment, with many single parents but also a high proportion of elderly people. In 1977 a local Community Council was formed by the Borough to try to develop a sense of community spirit. It organised various activities, such as carnivals and flower shows. In 1980–2 an inter-agency project in the area was felt to demonstrate the need for a Neighbourhood Office from which various agencies on the estate would operate and which would provide an accessible advice point for local residents. The Office would also become the base for the Community Council. An Urban Aid grant was successfully applied for and the Hilldon Neighbourhood Project was set up for a five-year period. Urban Aid funding was used to appoint a full-time project worker, responsible to the Community Council. The

Childrens Society created an additional three-year post to develop family support activities. This worker was not accountable to the Community Council but to the Project Leader of the Herding Project—also funded by the Childrens Society.

From the start, Hilldon experienced difficulties associated with this structure. The joint brief of the two project workers was never clearly specified: they felt that expectations and policies were unclear and this led to confusion in their own relationships. Further, the Community Council of local residents was weak and not really interested in managing the Centre or developing policies. The original purpose of housing outposts of the various statutory agencies appeared to have been forgotten and no other purpose replaced it. The Project's aims therefore remained very general:

- to encourage groups and individuals, to help them grow in confidence and skills;

- to encourage people to have their say on matters that affect them and the opportunity to take an active part in the things that affect their lives and way of living.

The Childrens Society ended funding in 1987 and the project was re-structured. The Neighbourhood Centre was reconstituted as a private company, with its own Local Management Committee registered with the Charity Commission and independent from the Community Council.

Meadow Centre

The remaining area of the town which was thought by the planners to need a family project was the Marsh estate—an area of mainly older council housing considered to have many needs and to lack provision. Attempts were made in 1983 and 1984 to obtain funds through Urban Aid, without success. However, a local group of councillors and officers persisted in fund-raising efforts, supported by the social services department, who suggested approaching the National Society for the Prevention of Cruelty to Children (NSPCC). Negotiations with the NSPCC continued for over a year: the local group wanted NSPCC funding for a neighbourhood project, while the NSPCC initially wanted to tie funding more specifically to work with child abuse, and felt that the project worker should also be part of a child protection team. Eventually agreement was reached on a two-year funding period with additional funding from Social Services. The project did not start in time for its activities to be included in this research, but the chair of the local management group was interviewed.

In its draft constitution, the aims are listed as:

• To alleviate poverty by opening and running a Family Centre which is open for the benefit of all local residents.

• To advance education by supporting a number of activities in the area for particular groups as resources allow e.g. children, youth, parents, elderly, unemployed.

• To involve residents in Marsh North in identifying and meeting local social, educational, health and material needs.

The Meadow Family Centre was planned to operate with one project worker, employed by the NSPCC, who was to facilitate the formation and maintenance of parents' self-help groups on the estate. The groups will have creches and will make their own decisions about what they will do, within the Centre's general objectives.

Home-Start

Home-Start differed from the other six family projects because it was not based in a local neighbourhood but was intended to serve families with defined needs throughout the town. It also differed in being a local branch of an organisation with a national identity.

The first steps towards setting up the Newpath Home-Start branch were taken in 1979, when a Steering Committee was set up, under the wing of the Standing Committee for Under-Fives. The Steering Committee had considerable difficulty in raising funds, but after an energetic public relations campaign was eventually successful in 1982.

The Acorn Project

The Acorn project had its origins in discussions between local health professionals and the then project leader at the Herding Family Centre. They identified a need to provide more specific help for families where pre-school children were showing signs of developmental delay. The project was set up essentially for children who were not mentally handi-capped but were exhibiting developmental problems, such as very poor co-ordination, failure to develop language, or failure to thrive. These children and their parents were felt to need something 'extra' to help them use ordinary community playgroups and nurseries. Acorn takes such children between the ages of 20 months and three years, and offers a day educational programme to them and their mothers, with home visiting support, for a year. By developing children's abilities and social skills, and mothers' confidence and parenting skills, Acorn hopes that children will be enabled to cope normally once they start school.

Acorn was set up in 1984 by the Children's Society, with health and social services funding, and staffed by nursery nurses, one of whom came from the Herding Centre. It had a neighbourhood catchment area. The original project is now set to expand on a number of different sites.

Summary

In summary, consideration of the history of the establishment of the Neighbourhood Family Projects suggests that the reasons given for their existence have changed over time. In the late 1970s and early 1980s, the focus was very much on the need for day care provision—for working parents as well as for so-called priority groups. The three first-established projects all had the provision of some form of day care as part of their remit. Experience showed the difficulties of offering 'combined' day care, with staff employed by different employers, with different objectives and different conditions of service. Thus there seems to have been a conscious move away from direct service provision as an objective of the family projects, while nursery classes continued as a separate responsibility of the Education Department.

Another early aim of several of the projects was to provide a neighbourhood base for outposted statutory services—a place where local people could get early advice and access to professionals before problems reached crisis point. We have already discussed some of the reasons why the social services department failed to move in this direction. It is also true that, once the projects were established, by no means all of them favoured 'open access' for statutory staff. However, some part of this objective was retained in all the projects with the provision of Advice Points specialising in welfare rights, but willing to give advice on other problems. These were staffed, not by professionals but by volunteers.

The projects had always included loosely-defined aims to do with community development—the fostering of self-help groups and the desire to advocate for the local community's needs. In more recent years these aims appeared to become predominant. However, there remained considerable uncertainty and vagueness as to what was expected of the projects by funders and professionals.

This chapter and the previous one have attempted to give the reader, in perhaps tedious detail, some understanding of the contrasting approach to family support in the two research areas. The next chapter gives a snapshot of the structure and functioning of the innovative family projects in Newpath, as they were in 1988, when observed by the researchers.

CHAPTER 5

The Operation of the Family Projects

This chapter describes how six of the seven family projects were operating when the research was carried out—Meadow Centre was not yet operational. The research worker (Sally Thorpe) visited all the projects to observe some of their activities, and carried out semi-structured interviews with the project leaders and the chairs of the management committees. Managers from Social Services, Health, Education and the national voluntary societies were interviewed, as were representatives from other relevant community agencies, such as the Voluntary Services Centre and the Pre-school Playgroups Association. The interviews were tape-recorded and subsequently transcribed.

Project Philosophy

As we have seen, the Neighbourhood Family Projects (NFPs) were set up with very general aims, to do with alleviating the effects of social disadvantage, or improving the quality of life for residents in local areas. Both Acorn and Home-Start were established with more specific aims and had more clearly-defined 'target' groups who were expected to benefit from their services. In an attempt to understand more about the underlying approach of the projects, the interview with leaders asked whether their project was mainly concerned with individuals, families or with the local community itself. All the projects saw themselves as concerned with families. Only one NFP leader saw her project as also concerned to take up issues that affected the local community.

None of the NFPs was focusing only or mainly on families with specific needs or problems: in theory at least, they were at the service of any local residents. There were no age criteria for users, and even the 'local residence' criterion was operated loosely. This openness and unwillingness to be tied down to a defined set of limited objectives could sometimes lead to feelings of confusion:

> In theory we are oriented to general community issues. But in practice we do spend more time than perhaps was planned with individuals. I feel I've done very little in dealing with wider community issues like lack of facilities,

campaigning for things. … We're a hotch potch. That's been a real problem as well. I feel nobody's quite sure and I'm not either whether my job is Centre based or whether I should be out there, how much of the individual work we should be doing. (NFP Project Leader).

On the whole, however, staff in the NFPs appeared convinced of the value of an 'open-door' approach, without predetermined specific goals or methods of work.

Its all about increasing people's awareness. Supporting and alleviating stress within families. We work on the basis that everyone's got something. We're here to bring out the skills that they've all got. We work in a two-way process with people—not only that we've got something to offer them but they've got something to offer us. When someone new comes in, she doesn't know the difference between staff and members, which is what we hope to achieve. (NFP leader).

We define as much of our work as educational as we do as welfare—both words are in our constitution. That's good to me because education is about people taking control of their own lives. Welfare is far more the old patronage image. We don't run classes but we see what we're doing as having an educative role in the community. I think we've got the balance right. It's important to give knowledge and information to people. (NFP leader).

People often come to us lacking in self-esteem, pretty down on their luck, and through involvement they grow in confidence, not in ability so much as in ability to express themselves. We hope to make opportunities for them to use their talents within the project and to move on beyond us. We've seen that happen and we would regard that as evidence that we're on the right lines. (NFP leader).

The two remaining family projects—Acorn and Home-Start—both had more specific aims, with limited target groups and definite age criteria. The Home-Start Organiser explained the project's reasons for not adopting an open-door approach as follows:

We've often thought about the emphasis of Home-Start and thought how wonderful it would be if it was a drop-in centre. But then it would make it estate-bound, we'd have to be more of a family centre and I think the home-visiting would take second place. … It might not reach so many people and would only reach the confident. Very few of our mums would easily go and use a service somewhere or to a family centre. They still have difficulties even coming to the Family Group where they're transported and know the volunteers.

Acorn used a set of predetermined techniques and methods of work, after individualised assessment of users' needs. Although Acorn was an innovative family project based in a local neighbourhood, it seemed thoroughly professional in spirit. Home-Start, however, did not see itself as using professional methods:

> I think it's befriending, always. We're not necessarily sorting out people's problems, we're not equipped to, but we're taking a new element to their lives, trying to enrich their lives really. That often makes problems copeable with, but we don't go in because of the problem. (Home-Start Organiser).

Evaluation

Although all the project leaders accepted the need to keep some statistics, none had the resources or time to engage in any systematic monitoring or evaluation of the project's work, though several had given the whole question of evaluation a good deal of thought. There was a certain scepticism about the value of 'headcounting', although, as one NFP leader put it:

> It's useful to be able to chuck numbers at the funders of the world.

This leader believed that the process of evaluation must be involved with and reflective of day-to-day practice. She had monitored the project's work over a four-week period and used the figures to stimulate the Management Committee to

> reflect on whether what we're actually doing is what we think we're doing and try and get them to express how they see the project, and define what they think is going on. Then we can put that against our aims as expressed in our constitution.

Acorn and Home-Start had both recently taken part in independently-run evaluation exercises. Acorn had modified its approach to parents in response to the independent researcher's findings that parents were somewhat confused over what was expected of them. Acorn was also hoping that an independent follow-up study would be made to assess the progress of their children in ordinary schools. Home-Start had internal processes of collecting and evaluating statistics on referrals, and had an internal review in 1986 of where the project was going:

> It was looking at all we did really, because it was impossible to do all we did and we were getting to crisis point. We had to decide to cut down on some of the provision, such as some of the groups for volunteers. We looked harder at refusing some referrals.

Newton had hired an outside consultant to lead an evaluation exercise that involved project staff, users and volunteers as well as representatives of funders and statutory agencies. This was seen as an opportunity to review the project's activities and generate ideas for the future.

Small family projects are unlikely ever to have the resources to engage in systematic evaluation on their own, and yet such exercises may be necessary for fruitful development. There may be a need for independent funding for this purpose.

Premises
The family projects occupied a variety of premises, acquired in different ways. Newton had a four-bedroomed, detached house which had been bought by the National Childrens Home. Hilldon had its own building, which it rented from the council. Ashgrove had just moved to new rented promises in a purpose-built Community Centre. Acorn had been given space in a local college. The rooms had been specially adapted and no rent was charged. A further advantage was that Acorn had free access to college facilities. All these projects considered their premises well adapted for their purposes, (though disabled people would have experienced problems in using some of them).

Home-Start experienced difficulties since it rented office space in a dilapidated building owned by a Trust whose future appeared unclear. It rented a church hall for its family group meetings. Only Herding, occupying a hut (a former classroom) rented from the Education Department, considered that its premises were definitely unsuitable, being too small for activities.

Staffing
Staff working in the family projects came from a variety of backgrounds and brought different qualifications and experience with them (Table 5i).

All but one staff members were female and none were from minority groups. Only one project (Herding) said it had a definite policy of employing local residents. This project, the longest established, was also unusual in that its leader had originally come to Herding as a user. She had become a volunteer and had then been seconded by the Childrens Society to a Certificate in Social Services course.

Activities
A detailed summary of the activities running in an average week in all the projects at the time of the research visit is contained in Appendix 1. The NFPs, with their broad aims and open-door policies, offered the widest range of activities. At the time of the research visit, the four NFPs then in operation were offering between 11 and 16 separate activities during the course of a normal week. Home-Start and Acorn, with their more specialised approaches, were offering three to four activities.

Table 5i
Paid Staff in the Family Projects

Project	No Paid Staff	Sex	Qualifications Represented	No Locally Resident	Duties
Herding	1 FT 5 PT	F	CSS PPA course Clerical	5	Co-Ordinator Fam. Proj. Wkr. Welfare Rights
Hilldon	2 FT 1 PT	F	Youth & Community Work	1	Leader Admin. Asst. Cleaner
Newton	2 FT 1 PT	M F	Child Care Cert. HND Management Studies	0	Senior Worker Proj. Worker Admin.
Ashgrove	3 FT 1 PT	F	Youth & Community Work	1	Leader Worker Admin. Cleaner
Home-Start	3 PT	F	CQSW Teaching Qual.	NA	Organiser Asst. Org. Secretary
Acorn	1 FT 4 PT	F	NNEB Art degree	0	Acting Leader Proj. Workers

In the Neighbourhood Projects, some activities were aimed at particular age-groups, or at one sex only. For example, all the projects offered at least one activity, such as a holiday play scheme or a creche, that was aimed at *young children.* The NFPs had differing policies on creche workers. Ashgrove paid a local co-operative to care for children whose mothers were attending groups or activities. Herding, Newton and Home-Start used volunteers, usually after training, as creche workers. Ashgrove felt that women should not be used as unpaid childcarers, and that the use of specialised workers also guaranteed high quality care for the children and avoided the problems caused by volunteers being ill or not turning up. When the researcher visited a creche at Ashgrove, the children were painting murals on walls and creating sticky pictures. Other projects felt there were advantages in using volunteers, in that it could help to improve parenting skills and the training provided an opportunity to share problems.

Home-Start saw its weekly Family Group as benefiting parents and children. About 25 families came each week.

So many were so isolated that they never went outside their door apart from to the shops. They lacked the confidence to go to normal community Mother and Toddler groups. The group is based on the Cope model, where there's craft work for those that want, which helps communication and helps them feel they've achieved. It also relieves the parents because we have playleaders ... playing with and stimulating the children.

Some of the projects offered *women-only activities*, even though this was sometimes felt to cause resentment in husbands. Herding offered Time Out For Women, a social evening for women of all ages away from the family, which was run by a staff member and the borough's Neighbourhood Worker, and attracted about 15 users on average. Hilldon put on WOMEN (Women On Mondays: Evading Noise), which had been running for some three years and had 15 to 20 regular users. It had been started by a local resident to give women a friendly, secure meeting place away from the pubs. It was currently managed by a users' committee.

All the projects, except Acorn, provided *social activities* such as coffee mornings which (except for the Home-Start Family Group) were open to any local resident. They provided opportunities for people to meet each other, relax in a friendly atmosphere, and perhaps find out more about other activities on offer. When the researcher visited the coffee morning at Herding, for example, she found 13 children and 18 adults. Two volunteers were putting a lot of work into buying and selling food, running a raffle and organising a weigh-in for regular attenders. They tried to keep records of attendance and made a small charge of 20 pence per family. All ages were represented with two grannies joining in easily. At Newton the main coffee morning had become so packed that several other, smaller groups had to be started in addition. When the researcher visited, the lounge was crammed with parents, with a creche in the back for their children. Volunteers and staff were handing out questionnaires about present and future activities, which would be discussed at future 'Evaluation Days'. Ideas were coming up such as a baby-sitting circle, more for the over-fives and evening meetings. Meanwhile in the corner a mother who felt very depressed talked endlessly to a worker.

All the NFPs offered a range of *advice services*, provided by a mix of staff and volunteers. The standard of advice-giving on welfare rights in the projects appeared very high, probably due to the training and back-up available from the Newpath Law Centre, which provided a nine-week course for volunteers. Law Centre staff were also providing specialist advice over the telephone to help volunteers in more complex cases.

At Hilldon, for example, there were two Advice sessions weekly at the main centre, and one at a subsidiary outpost. There were two volunteers on duty at the time of the research visit—a retired shop steward and a former accounts clerk. Both were local residents who had been involved with the Centre for about two years. They had a careful recording system and a built-in follow-up to check on the outcome for claimants. They had managed to build up a good relationship with the Social Security office, whose staff now sent a written response to all

Advice Point queries within a week. Tea was served to callers and children could be looked after so that parents could discuss the problem undistracted. The volunteers were able to provide a personal service, with callers encouraged to return and see the same person. This enabled claimants to gain confidence and knowledge gradually. The volunteers were very conscious of the need for confidentiality, especially as their callers might also be their neighbours.

Hilldon also provided a Housing Advice Point at its subsidiary centre in response to local demand revealed in a survey. The weekly sessions were run by an assistant from the Housing Department, with the help of a volunteer. The housing assistant told the researcher that he had managed this part of the estate for years and "they know I am the council". He was enthusiastic about the usefulness of the Advice Point in helping people who couldn't get to the office with problems over repairs, transfers or public health complaints. Six or seven people came each time. His liaison with the project and the research it had done had led to rubbish skips being provided on the estate and the appointment of a full-time caretaker.

Opportunities for the *exchange of resources* were seen as important by most of the NFPs: three provided ways in which their users could obtain direct access to resources. Ashgrove had a successful Thrift Shop, run mainly by volunteers. Users brought in good second hand clothes to sell and the centre kept 20 per cent of the proceeds. Apart from its value in providing cheap goods, the scheme had an important educational function as the volunteers were really running a small business. It was also seen as a good way of getting people into the centre. Herding was attempting a similar venture, but its unsuitable accommodation was proving a problem. Ashgrove and Hilldon also provided access to facilities that were otherwise hard to obtain on the estate—such as photocopiers, telephones or laundry equipment. Ashgrove aimed to provide cheap meals. A worker commented that some parents were not eating enough themselves, spending what they had on the children. At Newton there was a different policy. The project leader feared that the provision of material resources could make people dependent, and the project therefore preferred to concentrate on direct work with people through activities, information and support, encouraging them to take their own initiatives. Even here, however, volunteers and staff organised a successful holiday each year for families who otherwise would not have been able to afford one.

There was a variety of activities which could be seen as broadly *educational* in aim, such as volunteer training and support groups, Keep Fit, Relaxation Training, and adult literacy provision.

All the NFPs, as well as Home-Start and Acorn, awarded a high priority to supporting individuals (usually mothers) facing difficulties. Staff in all the family projects were spending a good part of their time in direct *counselling* as well as in supporting the volunteers who were giving a befriending service. This provision had sometimes changed its form over time. As one NFP leader put it in describing the project's Family Link scheme:

> It was originally seen as befriending for the isolated. It isn't the simple befriending we thought it would be. It can tend to be quite crisis-oriented and it's often on a referral basis from social services etc. It differs from Home-Start because it's not specifically for families with under-fives. It could be with an elderly person or a guy on his own.

This particular scheme currently had 33 self-referrals and 14 from the local authority, who were all getting help from four active volunteers and a paid worker who gave:

> counselling, for example with a family whose children have been taken away from them. It may develop into a friendship, and sometimes a referral (sic) has training and eventually becomes a volunteer. (NFP worker).

Users

All the projects kept some statistics, (such as numbers of referrals, attendance records at some groups, creche attendances) about their users, but they were of variable quantity and quality. Estimated numbers of weekly users are contained in the detailed summary in Appendix 1.

Only Ashgrove did not accept referrals from statutory agencies. The reasons for referral were similar in all the NFPs. At Newton, for example, the project leader felt the agency expected them

> usually to work with families whom they see as isolated in the community, who are under general family pressures. ... Usually to introduce them to a group so they meet other people. Sometimes there's a need for financial counselling. At the moment I pick up all the referrals—go and visit.

At Herding, the workers thought that families were referred for support.

> Part of it is they haven't had very good parenting themselves, it may be marital problems. You see when the social workers first make the referral to Family Link, they may just say the parent is isolated, she's had a breakdown of marriage, but one you actually go in there and regular support is given, you find out all sorts of other areas in which support is needed. It may be because of child abuse—children are on the at risk register. It may be somebody that's had a recent bereavement, but again on the referral form it may just say isolated.

At Hilldon, where there were no standard referral forms, the project leader felt that referring agencies just expected

> that we'll visit somebody to tell them about the neighbourhood centre.

At Ashgrove, no referrals were accepted. The project leader explained:

> We don't operate the sort of model where a family or a problem is processed. ... I don't let social services refer people to this centre. We don't accept referrals from any agency. If a social worker, aid, health visitor would want one of their clients to come they usually would check that out with us first, and what we would do then is explain our policy to them and we would say if you go back to your clients and tell them all about the centre and encourage them to come, that's fine. If they feel it would be useful to them that's fine. If they would like one of us to go and talk about the centre that's fine, but the decision is still theirs. And when they come along here they are treated exactly the same as anyone else.

In practice, therefore, Ashgrove may not have differed that much from the other NFPs, in that workers called on parents whom agencies had referred, with their permission, to introduce themselves and discuss what the project offered. However, Ashgrove was prepared to set boundaries around its work and challenge workers from statutory agencies to a greater extent than were the other family projects.

We asked all project leaders if certain kinds of users might be excluded, as too difficult for the project to deal with, giving the examples of serious marital problems, physical illness, money problems, children at risk of physical injury or sexual abuse, serious trouble with the law. No project admitted excluding any category of user. But as the Herding leader pointed out,

> Although we say this is open to everyone in the community there are lots of things that stop people coming in here. They may be in a wheelchair, they could come in but they couldn't go to the toilet.

Several projects felt they were used by too few people and would have liked to attract more, while recognising the limits imposed by space and resources. All had produced publicity material about their activities, and the NFPs and Home-Start engaged in a good deal of activity to publicise themselves by, for example, door-to-door leafletting, local press and radio advertisement, posters in shops and libraries. Word-of-mouth, however, was generally felt to be the best method of recruitment. Activities themselves, as we have seen, were often a way of drawing in new people.

The researcher's impression, from visiting the projects, was that users were overwhelmingly drawn from the ranks of white women and their children. All the projects agreed that there were some gaps in their coverage. The most commonly mentioned was the failure to attract any users from ethnic minority groups (though the proportion in the local population was small). The absence of disabled or older people was also mentioned by some projects. As one leader put it, it's not good enough just to set up facilities. You've got to look at why disabled people or minority groups don't use them. You've got to be more active, more focused in how you advertise. That's a question of time. We haven't attempted it.

All agreed that men were notable by their absence. Some leaders believed that if more male staff were appointed to the projects, the proportion of male users would rise. Others felt that they couldn't expect to attract many men, since men would feel awkward about coming in because of stereotyped attitudes about 'women's matters', or attitudes that support was only needed by women.

Volunteers

All the project leaders were asked whether their project used volunteers. All except Acorn did so. In order to avoid over-stating their numbers, each individual volunteer was listed during the research interview. The results, as shown in Table 5ii are impressive, particularly as the projects were recruiting from local neighbourhoods generally thought of as disadvantaged—not the kinds of area where voluntary work has traditionally flourished.

The great majority of volunteers were white, working class women from local neighbourhoods. The age-range was wide, though most were in their thirties or forties. Home-Start had two volunteers from ethnic minority groups and Hilldon had one. Volunteers were performing a range of different tasks, depending on the structure of the project.

Table 5ii
Volunteers Working in the Family Projects

Project	Number	Local	Sex	Age-Group	Time	Tasks
Herding	34	All	F	21–65	1M–6Y	Befriending Running creches
Ashgrove	15	13	3M	20s–60s	1M–2Y	Welfare Rights Play scheme Thrift shop
Hilldon	11	10	3M	20s–60s	1M–3Y	Welfare Rights Reception duties
Newton	30	All	F	20–50	NK	Running creches Befriending Welfare rights Toy library Outings/holidays Running groups
Home-Start	58	NA	1M	20s–70s	NK	Befriending Family Group

Not all the project leaders were happy with the idea of the 'volunteer' as distinct from other users of the project. As the Ashgrove leader put it,

> We don't use volunteers. Everybody who comes to this centre mucks in. This centre is run entirely by its users and so in a way everyone's a volunteer and nobody's a volunteer. However having said that, there are a couple of groups or activities that run where the people involved are called volunteers. One day you could be here as a volunteer and the next day you're here as a user and you're performing essentially the same role—taking part in the running of the centre.

Hilldon, similarly, did not seem to define users who were running groups as 'volunteers'. Other projects, such as Newton and Home-Start, made clearer distinctions between the role of user or client and that of volunteer, although people could 'move on' from one to the other. The projects providing a befriending service seemed the more likely to demarcate the role of volunteer.

Apart from Ashgrove, all the projects undertook regular recruitment drives for new volunteers, through advertising and publicity or personal contact. Only Herding felt there were no real supply problems. Those projects which kept figures felt that turnover was very low—once volunteers were successfully inducted they tended to stay for relatively long periods. No project paid volunteers but all met out-of-pocket expenses. Volunteers from all the projects had moved on to paid work, more often outside the project than with it. This was usually seen as desirable. As the Home-Start Organiser said,

> We see that as a positive thing. They're like the families. They've got their families off to school and are looking for a role for themselves but lacking confidence, so it's a building of confidence through Home-Start. We always make a fuss of those who move on, and let everyone know. Volunteers come back for years to see us, which means that they feel it's OK to leave.

In all the projects, volunteers had to undergo some training. For the Advice Points, this was provided by the Law Centre. Otherwise the project leader was usually responsible for organising an internal training programme. Home-Start's was the most structured, consisting of a basic course of preparation, held on one day a week for a term, and covering the Home-Start approach, some basic child development, an understanding of relationships, and resources in the community. All the projects provided continuing supervision and support for their volunteers, both individually and in groups.

Management Structures

The projects were managed in a variety of ways, with the most interesting and contentious model being the Local Management Committee (LMC). For the purposes of this discussion, we may think of management responsibilities as involving the hiring and firing of staff, responsibility for the building, for finances, and for policies. Using this rough definition, the responsible authorities were as shown in Table 5iii.

Table 5iii
Management of the Family Projects

Local Management Committee	Childrens Society	National Childrens Home	NSPCC
Hilldon	Acorn	Newton	Meadow
Ashgrove		(plus Advisory	(plus Local Management
—Herding—		Committee)	Committee)
Home-Start			

Herding was in process of moving from management by the Children's Society to management by a local committee. At Meadow there was a strong local committee, with responsibilities for managing finances and the building, but the NSPCC continued to employ the project worker. Thus there were three broad patterns of management at the time of the research: by a local management committee; by a voluntary society; or by a mixture of the two. Since full-blown local management represented the most exciting development, and the one which posed the most obvious problems, it is worth considering in more detail.

Local Management

The Local Management Committees (LMCs) had a similar structure, with a Chair, sometimes a Vice-Chair, a Secretary and Treasurer. These might be elected or recruited locally for their suitability and then formally elected. Then in the NFPs there were between five and eight elected local people, some of whom were representing users, or particular user groups. Home-Start had two elected volunteer representatives. Funding agencies all had representatives on the management committees (usually without a vote) and there were also co-opted members. Social Services was represented on every LMC; Health and Education on most. The Borough Community Development Team was represented at Hilldon and Ashgrove. Local councillors were co-opted members and one played a particularly important role at Herding. Thus the committees consisted essentially of local people, often without previous similar experience, who were office-holders and voting members; and agency and political representatives who were usually non-voting members. Legally, Ashgrove, Hilldon and Herding were Limited Companies.

A project leader described the advantages and problems of this structure as follows:

> Having a LMC is a real plus to the Neighbourhood Centre in terms of local accountability and control, but I don't think enough thought went into supporting and training the committee. There was a feeling that my job was to support them, which is absolutely impossible, you can't do it when you're employed by them. The personnel changed quite quickly. With a lot of local committees, when you rely on volunteers, people's circumstances change, they're no longer able to give as much involvement, so there was quite a turnover. You have to keep re-explaining the whole time what the project is about. And as you get new people, their priorities change and you seem to be continuously changing aims.

However, this worker felt that the committee started to work better when it was re-structured to give more representation to users of the centre, who had a real stake in decisions.

The causes of difficulty most often mentioned, from the point of view of project workers, seemed to be the committee members' lack of experience in and unpreparedness for, the role of employers; their lack of time; conflicts within the committee; rapid turn-over; and lack of opportunities for members to train and develop. As we shall see in a later section, the Newpath Voluntary Services Centre, in spite of its own limited resources, had stepped into the gap and attempted to provide training and support for new committee members. The professional most involved had a clear view of the problem:

> The worker often has the double bind of both doing the work and sustaining a management group to manage. It's almost an impossible load. ... The MC has the responsibility to support the worker, and they're not very skilled at doing that but don't necessarily know how to negotiate outside support. At the same time the worker is quite clearly supporting the MC through their management role. A lot of groups haven't any idea what responsibilities they're taking on—premises, insurance, legal responsibilities, the responsibilities are enormous. You have to be realistic about how much time committee members can give to training though they know they need the skills for the job. The turnover is enormous. No sooner have you got a group of people who seem to be on top of it than you've got another group. And often training can be quite a disabling thing because it throws up all the things they don't know. ... Don't get me wrong. I'm not against LMCs and local control. You can see there's tremendous space for personal growth. But it depends on a lot of input from people to sustain it. And that's not appropriate work for a worker within a project. The statutory workers who go on MCs who could perhaps be a resource if they had the skills themselves,

really aren't independent enough … because they bring the funders' perspectives. It would be too controlling. They are better used developing the ideas about partnership and being aware when a voluntary organisation is being unduly put upon by a statutory authority or having its work distorted. You almost need a fulltime resource person … from outside.

Most project leaders had access to independent professional consultation and did not rely solely on the support of their management committees.

The challenge of local management was being most acutely experienced at Herding, where the Childrens Society was in process of pulling out of its former funding and management commitments. The present project workers described 'the bombshell' that had burst around them—the volunteers (as they then were).

> The Childrens Society were saying they were actually moving out of … they called this 'old work'—family centres—they were moving on to other new initiatives. I think they felt that the family centres had actually proved themselves and therefore they were looking towards other people like the county council to take on the funding. … It was a shock to find out that we were going to be responsible for this building when none of us had any training. The main feeling was, why haven't we been informed and trained up. … We were being told, there's going to be no staff there, you're going to be doing it yourselves. The original staff team had not been told they would only be in there for four or five years. As far as they were concerned they were going to be here for ever and ever. So it was a big shock.

The Childrens Society, at the time of the research, were still providing training costs and administering the funding, but they were shortly to withdraw. The workers were coping with many difficulties and described how they had rapidly had to acquire skills in fund-raising:

> A worker is having to be laid off. It causes problems for the LMC and staff not having had to do this before [i.e. raise money]. We have got the skills now because we had to do it for the application to Allied Dunbar, but we didn't know we had that till we actually sat down—a whole week wasn't it? We did it as a team. We did it on our own initiative, we didn't have any help. We had to have things like job descriptions which I didn't have. … That's where we found out that the wages being asked for weren't enough to cover the new position. … Last week was really bad. I got a letter about my redundancy and I think it finally hit me then that I wouldn't be here in two weeks time. … Communication with them as employers is very difficult. We've just felt very unsupported in this.

The then regional manager of the Childrens Society explained to the researcher that the national agency had changed its strategy, partly on the basis of lessons learned in Newpath. While the original intention had been to remain permanently, now the Society wished to get out of the centre as soon as possible, but leaving it strong and healthy, staffed by local people and funded by local statutory agencies. He explained that,

> the style now is that we appoint community development people because we believe that the bulk of it is community development not social work, that's the model we'd like. We have appointed different staff in five parts of the region now, community development teams to work across a diocese of the Church of England and Church of Wales on a contract basis, time-limited work, which could be a parish ringing up saying 'we'd like a family centre, can you help us develop it?' In which case one of our staff would be committed for three to six months to help develop a family centre. We would then withdraw and be available to provide the same service elsewhere.

The regional manager considered that family centres would actually benefit from the Childrens Society's removal, since it would "remove the shackles of being child-oriented" and allow centres to market services for other client groups—such as the mentally ill and handicapped and the elderly. This might ensure them an increased grant from statutory authorities.

In spite of the stresses, the Herding staff took a positive view of local management. The new committee had been successfully elected, and although at first there was a problem with people leaving because they were overwhelmed by what was expected, the committee was now looking more settled.

What were the views of the LMC members themselves? The chairpersons interviewed usually had clear views of the committee's functions:

> The MC is ultimately responsible for the direction of the project and the funding. It must have an important role in monitoring the expenditure. It's responsible for the building. And hiring and firing.
>
> We are employing the staff and we should be responsible for the work environment and the nitty gritty of employment. Taking management policy decisions.
>
> The committee's function is to manage both finance and the events that take place. It doesn't mean running them, but knowing what goes on. We're responsible for the actual building. At the moment we're not in the hiring and firing. ... To be quite honest that's the bit that I don't really feel I would like, to be someone's employer. To me it's horrifying to have the responsibility. ... It's the confidence in that part of it that I'm lacking.

The chairs all saw the responsibilities of the management committee in much the same way, though some spoke more openly than others about their hesitations in assuming them. However, they differed more in their views of the role of the chairperson, differences which no doubt reflected the fact that there may be more than one way of playing this particular role successfully. Chairs usually seemed to be appointed or elected by members of the committee, or persuaded to take on the role, rather than elected at an Annual General Meeting. This was felt to be an advantage:

> It's good that the MC elect their own chair. I've actually seen at a general meeting a chairman get elected because of the amount of people he promised drinks in the bar. ... I see an influx of about 50 people and they just voted and then went back into the bar. They didn't take part in the meeting and didn't worry about the meeting.

Some chairs saw themselves as essentially mediators and enablers, 'standing alongside' staff. Others took a more hands-on position:

> I certainly don't think that a chair should be, you know, controlling or directive. I think ideally the chair should be someone who is involved but who is enabling. ... The chairperson is in quite a good position to be a sort of mediator. But also enough involved to be able to ask questions which need asking, which could be of the staff or of the participants.
> Chairing the meeting, see the agenda is prepared, that the meeting starts on time, make sure the points are kept to, that everyone gets a fair share of putting their views in discussion. ... As a Chair I sort of sit back, you don't have your own views do you? You've got to be impartial. Open mind. Signing letters. The representative I suppose.
> In one way, an overseer I suppose, to see that the Neighbourhood Worker is doing their job right. ... To try and guide the Management Committee but to take instructions from them. ... Any problems, I'm the first person that gets the blame. If I make a decision and they decide not to support it, I'm in the wrong. But if they want to tie my hands up by saying you must consult the whole of the committee, then things that go wrong will get worse. So I said I wasn't going to have my hands tied. If someone comes to me with a problem, I've got to be able to solve it there and then.

Chairs usually felt that the composition of the committee—the balance and interests represented on it—was right, at least in theory. But it was sometimes difficult to persuade members to take an active interest and attend regularly. This was felt to be a drawback in the case of potentially useful members, such as local politicians.

> We don't have any councillors who come regularly and that's a pity. The councillor we did have wasn't re-elected unfortunately, and we've just not been able to nobble someone else. [Why is a friendly councillor an advantage?] Money! It would be good to have a county councillor who attended fairly regularly. They can speak in committee and support the project.

Sometimes the composition of the committee and its officers posed tricky problems for the Chair, who needed political guile:

The Vice Chair is my wife. ... I'm not happy with the position I'll be quite honest with you. It was actually a very peculiar situation last meeting. We had a vote on the re-election of the officers for three months. It was the Chair's casting vote. I declined to use it. I know both people personally. The person standing was a very old friend—an ex-girl friend my best friend pinched off me—and of course my wife's the Vice Chair. So if I made a decision between the two of them it's Catch 22 sort of thing. So I pushed it over to an article I've got in the file on how the Chair does his job. The Chair should always maintain the status quo and let the committee make the decision. So I maintained the status quo.

Chairs tended to feel that the main problem with the composition of their committees was the lack of people with specific management skills. As one Chair put it:

We are basically a group of carers with none of these sort of personnel skills.

Some Chairs expressed the view that the representatives from statutory authorities who were on their committees might supply this lack, and that it might be helpful if authorities would choose representatives with management skills, rather than fieldworkers.

The management committees have got to bring in people with the skills that they lack. And if they only way is through the statutory authorities making, not their fieldworkers but their administrative staff available—but then committees may feel wary of that, feeling checked up on, but if you've really got a partnership then you can accept that role from them. People who know about the whole bit of employing people, knowing about salaries and pensions and all the rest of it, and holidays. I mean if you could see me trying to work out what holiday allowance they should have—but it's quite wrong that the workers themselves should be working out what their holiday allowance is—I had to go round and find out how to do it.

No Chair expressed the view that representatives from the statutory authorities, or the funders, were having too much influence on the committee's deliberations or trying to control policy. If anything, they felt left too much to their own devices. However, some did draw attention to communication problems between professional representatives and local committee members.

X tends to talk too high. ... I think he's losing some of his reality with the public, he's losing that common ground language. I mean you don't start using big words. If you have big words, don't use them, especially with this committee. ... They're the people that read the Sun. X is the people that read the Times. ... It's the language that he's using. It's too high for the people.

In summary, therefore, Chairs were committed to the idea of local management, valued their projects' independence from control of statutory authorities and national voluntaries, and the local accountability that it promised. At the same time they felt the lack of specific skills and expertise to fulfil the role of employers, and also realised that their committees would inevitably have a frequently changing membership so that skills would have to be relearned again and again. Two different ways were suggested of compensating for this lack of management training and experience. One view was that the statutory authorities should supply skilled administrators to sit on the individual LMCs. The other view was that an independent body, such as the Newpath Voluntary Services Centre, might be given funding to organise a management service that projects could share. Chairs took their responsibilities very seriously and were conscious that the failure of local management could mean that projects would founder:

> I wouldn't like to think we were going to muddle along. I'd like to think we were going to do it in a professional way, because [the committees] are very important. I don't think it will be successful if you just muddle along. I think you've got to know what you're doing, you've got to be confident in what you're doing. Until you've got [the responsibilities] right in your mind they are a bit of a burden. Which could, after a while, reflect on the good parts of the centre. Your confidence would probably go to the extent where you'd think, I've had enough, why bother?

External Relations

1. Relations With Other Agencies

The six operational family projects were connected with a wide range of other agencies in Newpath, in the voluntary and statutory sectors. The main 'referring' agencies were Health and Social Services, and we shall examine these contacts in a little more detail.

Health-based professionals had the closest relationships with Home-Start and Acorn. As we have seen, both these projects had a 'service' philosophy and were working largely with referred clients. Thus their relationships with referring agencies, of which Health was predominant, appeared close and usually uncomplicated—although health visitors were not always good at making referrals and sometimes tended to 'overpersuade' families who subsequently backed out. Health visitors were never seen as shedding the responsibility for families they had referred. Projects did not have 'link' health visitors and did not seem to have many contacts other than for referral purposes.

A community health services manager considered that projects like Acorn and Home-Start fitted the policy guidelines for Health funding, in that they were either providing a substitute service; or they were operating in areas (development of under-fives) that directly concerned the Health Service. It might be possible in the future to develop other kinds of relationship with the neighbourhood centres, for example by basing some health clinics there; or by developing links around the concept of health education.

Contacts between the family projects and social services were also mainly concerned with making and receiving referrals (except in the case of Ashgrove which refused on principle to be part of a formal referral system). Contacts were most often described as being between the project leader and the referring social worker, though contacts with managers did take place at meetings or, in some cases, on the management committees. All the projects except Ashgrove said they received referrals, and all six said they made referrals. Most expressed themselves as quite satisfied with referral arrangements and with the agency's behaviour after a referral had been made. Only one project stated that social services was using it to shed their own responsibilities.

All the projects who took part in a referral system had clear rules protecting confidentiality, and none would visit a family who had not already been informed of the referral and given their consent. On the whole, referrals were considered appropriate, although with some exceptions:

> I had one for a young girl, they said she'd like to come and work in the creche and when I went to visit her she was in a wheelchair and although she'd like to work with children she knows there's no way she can. In talking to her I discovered that what she wanted was to maybe work in a shop in town like the Spastics Society. So it was really about getting her in touch with where she really needed to be and just get back to social services and say this is what I've done. ... Otherwise outside agencies hear you have volunteers and think that volunteers may do anything. There was a gentleman that wanted his trousers put on every morning.
>
> Generally speaking there are no problems. However there have recently been two very strange referrals, inappropriate. One from a duty officer, declined to give their name, tried to persuade us to do an emergency intervention which isn't our role.
>
> The problems come in seeing [project] as a dustbin or a last resort—what else can we do with the family, we've tried everything else. But we have no problems in saying, this is not for us.

Projects were aware of the pressure on the social workers in Newpath, where there was a staff shortage at the time of the research, and their expectations of the department were limited. One project leader, however, clearly expected to be treated as a professional colleague and saw his project as constituting part of a 'package' of services that might be offered to a family.

The key thing I'm trying to say is I want them to recognise the respective roles possible ... Social Services often see themselves as carrying cases in isolation. Yet from my point of view a lot of my work is about trying to tie up the various groups of people involved. I'm actively trying to get groups of people into some kind of communication about the particular situation.

Other project leaders seemed to see themselves as interpreters, making it easier for families to use social services, and helping social workers to gain acceptance:

We hear people say, social workers take your kids away. I think that's one of the things we're working—One of the things for me. I came here as a user, then a worker, then when I [did a course] people here would say, what are you going to be at the end of the day? And I'd say it's a social work qualification. And they'd say ugh, a bloody social worker [laughs]. But then they'd say, but you're alright. And then to say to them, but that's what it's about, it's because you don't know them personally. ... Knowing me in the past and knowing me now they can actually make comparisons and say, they're not starched figures, they are people with families of their own, and past experiences too, not always good.

Ashgrove was alone in wanting to "keep social services just about at arms length". This was the policy of the LMC, which the project workers faithfully implemented. Referrals were not accepted, and social workers were not allowed free access to the centre—they could not just drop in without invitation. On the other hand, this was the one centre where there was a named 'link' social worker. The project leader thought this was a good idea, since the link helped the social worker to understand the estate better:

She can use her local knowledge to help keep families together. Her judgments about whether things will work or not are much better because she knows the local family structures, and it's also useful that she knows how this place operates, all that helps her in making social work decisions about individuals. She also informs the team. Fights the cause of neighbour-hood centres.

Ashgrove, therefore, did not want to cut itself off from statutory social services, but it did seem to have a different view from the other projects of what a productive relationship should be. Links should not involve discussions about the needs of individual families but rather concern issues affecting families in the local area. However, there did seem to be difficulties in creating links of this kind:

There is a need to liaise with professionals working in the area, and a strong case for things like professional lunches because there is an advantage in knowing about each other's area of work and where they overlap. ... We tried to set up links with the team covering the area but re-organisation put the lid on that. It seemed there would be a benefit in going and meeting the team. We tried to set it up and then they re-organised into four new teams. It's still sort of on the agenda. I don't even know, apart from [link worker] who's in the Children and Families team. I would like that to come from social services, you know, a piece of paper arrive on my desk, For Your Information these are the members of the team and these are their extension numbers. ... I would like information about how often team meetings are held, that sort of thing would be a real bridge-building exercise, a way of being able to use what's there.

Another NFP leader expressed rather similar ideas about the difficulty of making links with social services, other than those directly concerned with referred families.

In a general way I'm not very satisfied with the way they work. Not just in particular cases. I just don't feel there's that much interest. They may see us as a local resource but they don't see us as another agency that they can do joint work with. ... We set up a scheme for teenagers which was supposed to be in partnership with them and that's the only example of what I consider joint work is about. I wouldn't just want to get lists of names from them. We could have identified a need together.

A senior social services manager, however, believed that it was easier to obtain funding for voluntary family centres than to fund preventive work with families within social services itself. He believed that the value of the family projects to the social services department was,

to provide a non-stigmatised form of intervention, and the other thing is to allow people within the communities and neighbourhoods to define their own problems and how they are going to deal with them. The bottom line is to keep people, if possible, away from our services and allow the family centres to nip family situations in the bud so that children don't enter the social services system which softens them up for care.

In addition, he believed that the family centres were contributing to facilities for young children in areas where the playgroup movement often found it hard to get established. This manager agreed that links between the projects and the social services department needed to be re-thought. He considered that team leaders were the appropriate link people, since one of the main purpose of any links should be to work with the family centre in drawing up a neighbourhood profile—"seeing what the referrals are, how they can help us out, all that sort of thing". By improving communication he hoped better mutual understanding could be achieved:

I don't think you can fund people and then stipulate their agenda. They have to define their agenda, but it's legitimate for our department to have an interest which you push at them but which they can push back at you in a different form. I think you can outline the problem but not the solution. ... We can give them our view of the problems and we can also tell them about our problems working in their areas and then it's up to them. I wouldn't want to control. I think that's the whole point with voluntaries—that if you tell them what to do you might as well do it yourself.

It seemed that relations between the neighbourhood family projects and both Health and Social Services were in a transitional stage. As we have seen, the social services Area director had played a very large part in the establishment of the projects. Perhaps the great effort needed made it hard to give time simultaneously to developing policies for the appropriate relationship between statutory and voluntary preventive work. Probably, it was only when projects had been running long enough to establish their own constituencies and ways of working that 'partnership' became at all feasible. For whatever reason, the two sides were only at the beginning of the process of clarifying expectations and developing policies to guide their relationship for the future. An important issue for the neighbourhood family projects seemed to concern the right balance of their work between the needs of individual families in distress, and the needs of families in general on their particular estates. There was little sign that the NFPs were yet becoming involved in broader issues that affected families in general—such as day care or playgroup provision for example—or even in issues that affected families in need as a group—such as their treatment by statutory agencies, for example.

Funders
At the time of the research, funding for several of the projects had reached a critical stage. This report therefore reflects some of the uncertainty and confusion that was being experienced in the projects.

As the Social Services Community Development Officer put it,

in a context where each authority has to go back and account to quite different systems—and that's one of the complexities, there are different cycles for each agency—different processes and different criteria, and that it's worked at all is probably amazing.

Funding for most projects had to be applied for annually. Although a guide to help voluntary organisations through the system had recently been produced by the main statutory funders, this system itself was generally recognised to be unsatisfactory. Efforts were being made to establish a three-year rolling cycle of funding, with agreements so that all organisations knew what the money was for, what expectations were attached to it, and what leeway they had to do other things, outside the specified purposes. It was hoped that a number of pilot agreements on these lines would be tested shortly. This would represent a move towards 'contracting out' of specified tasks or services, but all those concerned were anxious to preserve the autonomy of the voluntary sector to operate in its own way.

Although a three-year funding cycle would provide more stability and security for the voluntary sector, the general political climate posed considerable threat. The county's financial position was likely to be adversely affected by the imposition of the poll tax (community charge); and the borough was severely affected by rate-capping. In the future, therefore, these important funding agencies might be facing a choice between supporting their own staff in post, and continuing to support the voluntary sector. The commitment from the national voluntary societies was also far from permanent. We have already described the effects of the Childrens Society's withdrawl from Herding NFP. The National Childrens Home was still standing firm in Newton, but its regional manager pointed out some of the problems, from his point of view:

> I'm very happy to see if our work goes into a local authority, or into local groups, but what we can't do is say that the money we have committed to it will continue when we withdraw. The group has got to find an alternate form of funding for the contribution we have made. I believe it is absolutely right for a voluntary agency to demonstrate the need for, to establish, a form of operational work and to pass it on to someone else. ... We can go on giving oversight and managerial support but what we can't do is give that amount of our financial commitment to another agency to do work that we've done in the past. One of my great worries is that so many of these local projects become so big that it is impossible for the sort of money to be raised locally.

In other words, if the Newton centre were to pass to the control of a local management group, like the other NFPs, the National Childrens Home would be unable to continue its funding. Since the agency had not been able to find anyone to take over the full cost, it thought it wrong to abandon the project to its fate. The NSPCC had perhaps found an acceptable compromise in its lengthy negotiations with the new Meadow centre, whereby it employed the project worker, with full managerial control, but also co-operated with a local management committee who handled the social services grant, and took responsibility for the building.

The views of project leaders about their funding were sought during the research interview. All the projects on a one year funding cycle considered that this period was too short and that it posed many administrative and planning difficulties. All the projects except Acorn and Newton (both still the direct responsibility of national voluntaries) express-ed considerable fears for the future. Only these two projects were satisfied with the actual process of applying for funding. However these were also the only projects that thought the funders had some influence on the way their projects were managed, who used the projects, and the kinds of activities that were provided. No projects complained of interference on the part of funders, and most considered that funders exercised little or no influence on the actual operation of the project.

It is perhaps ironic that Newpath, which pioneered collective development within a strong commitment to partnership between statutory and voluntary organisations, should now find itself beginning to develop funding arrangements with the voluntary sector which may not be so far removed from newer ideas of 'contracting-out' welfare provision. Whether Newpath could continue its pioneering role in preventive family work within the new climate was not clear. Funders tended to express some optimism that, provided the statutory sector was able to maintain its present funding levels—by no means certain—Newpath would continue to point the way to pluralism, choice and local accountability; and that the new funding procedures, with their more precise statement of expectations and obligations, would not undermine the autonomy and flexibility of the voluntary sector.

Newpath Voluntary Services Centre: The Intermediary Role
From the early days of the family projects, the Voluntary Services Centre (VSC) played an important co-ordinating role in their development. It was well-suited to play the role envisaged by the Wolfenden Committee (1978) for 'local intermediary agencies'. It had an active directorate, a resource centre and hosted a community work student unit. The then Coordinator was very aware of potential differences of interests between providers and receivers of services, and between the voluntary sector and the local authority. The role of the VSC was to provide information and backup to voluntary groups; to act as a focus for development and training; and to promote communication and liaison.

In Newpath, however, some of these roles were less clear because of the commitment within the borough to community development. In some respects the roles of the borough's Community Development Team and the VSC overlapped. The present Coordinator expressed the view that there was some danger in thinking of the VSC as a 'neutral' co-ordinating body. He pointed out that VSC itself was in competition with other voluntary bodies for funding. Sometimes other groups might see it as self-interested and too powerful.

The Coordinator considered that the main contribution of the VSC was in bringing the various funders together with each other and with the projects themselves and promoting dialogue. This was achieved through the Family Projects Policy and Liaison Group, whose meetings took place at VSC.

The VSC was also instrumental in the institution of joint annual 'day seminars' for all the projects and representatives of the funders. These annual events were important both as a means of preventing the Projects from becoming isolated, and as a means of informing influential funders about their work. The head of the student unit at first acted as the central organiser for these programmes, and chaired the events themselves. However, by 1988 the Neighbourhood Family Projects Workers Group was confident enough to take on the coordinating role for any future inter-project events, with the support of Local Management Committees. A Conference and Liaison Fund, administered by VSC was established with annual contributions from statutory and voluntary funders of the Projects.

The early annual seminars were concerned with the production of an agreed Statement on the purposes and structure of the projects, which went some way to clarifying the expectations of the funders and allowed local management to move ahead in most of the projects (see Appendix 1).

Another area of VSC involvement was more specifically concerned with training and development, especially in relation to the newly established Local Management Committees. For example, the VSC Training and Development Worker held six-monthly consultancy sessions with the Herding Project; she worked for a year with the new Local Management Committee at Ashgrove to help them work out their roles and training needs and with the conduct of their meetings; she acted as a resource for the Hilldon LMC in a similar way. However, it was not possible or desirable to maintain this level of support without a clearer contract between funders and the VSC, and this had not yet been negotiated at the time of the research.

There appeared to be definite advantages in having these 'brokering' and development functions performed by a voluntary agency which saw itself in an intermediary position, rather than by a statutory agency such as the social services department.

PART 3

FAMILIES IN TWO AREAS:

Problems, Services and Outcomes

CHAPTER 6

Methods of the Family Surveys

Questions

Part 2 described different approaches to the provision of family support, and how new resources had been developed in local areas. Part 3 turns to families themselves. Research surveys were planned to explore parents' own views of their problems and needs for support, and the use they made of community resources.

These questions were investigated through three linked surveys of parents:

- a randomly selected sample of parents living in Newpath in the areas surrounding the new family projects;

- a sample of parents from the same areas referred to Newpath social services;

- a sample of parents referred to social services in the comparison area of Oldweigh.

A series of questions was posed:

1. How exceptional were families referred to social services? Did they differ markedly from other families living in similar areas in family structure, or levels of problem, or degree of isolation from sources of support?

2. Where did ordinary families turn for help and support? What use did they make of informal sources of support (family, friends and neighbours) as compared with formal services or locally-based alternatives? How did they use locally-based family projects?

3. What did families expect from supportive services? How satisfied were they with the help on offer?

4.   What problems did referred families present to the social services
     department, and what help did they obtain? Did families' problems
     change as a result?

5.   To what extent were social workers aware of, and willing to use,
     voluntary family support projects? In particular, were there differences
     between Newpath, where there was a network of neighbourhood
     family projects as well as a generally vibrant voluntary sector, and
     Oldweigh? For example, the pattern of referrals might differ: if the
     new projects were providing local advice services, workers in Newpath
     might be receiving more selective referrals of more serious problems.
     Workers in Newpath might be more knowledgeable about, and make
     more use of voluntary support resources; and spend more time in
     community activities. Families in Newpath might more often be
     linked into voluntary groups as a result of referral, and might find it
     easier to resolve their family difficulties because of the greater availabil-
     ity of social support.

Methods

Drawing the Community Sample

An agency (Public Attitude Surveys Ltd) was commissioned to undertake
a local population sample survey in Newpath of families containing
children under 14. Unfortunately, resources did not permit community
surveys in Oldweigh as well as Newpath. The person interviewed was
the parent most responsible for day-to-day care of the children. This was
nearly always the mother. The structured interview schedule was developed
for the Community and Referral Surveys by the author and tested in pilot
work by the agency. The experienced interviewers underwent a preliminary
training period.

A random sample of addresses from the four postcode areas surrounding the family projects in Newpath was drawn by computer, using a
listing of electoral registers. Addresses of families included in the (previously drawn) sample of social services referrals were excluded. Interviewers
on the doorstep then identified families who had children of the right age.
Although a random sample of 1,750 addresses was drawn, only 24 per
cent of them proved to contain children under 14. Thus three-quarters of
the addresses visited were not eligible to take part in the study. Only 230
interviews instead of the desired 400 were achieved by this sampling
method. In order to complete the survey within the time allowed,
interviewers had to be allowed to go to the two adjacent addresses on
either side if the sampled address proved ineligible. Interviewers were *not*
allowed to take adjacent addresses when the sample address was eligible.

There is no reason to suppose that bias has been introduced since the adjacent addresses were in similar property in the same small area. By this means 129 interviews were added, giving 359 completed interviews.

The overall rate of successful interviews from the originally drawn sample of addresses known to contain children under 14 was 77 per cent. The refusal rate was 21 per cent, and in a further two per cent the main caregiver could not be contacted. In 71 cases, no contact was achieved after four calls. It is not known how many of these addresses contained 'eligible' families.

In a further analysis, the addresses were grouped into six small areas. There was no difference between the areas in the proportions of interviews successfully completed, suggesting that bias from different local patterns of response was not a problem.

The Referral Samples
During an initial pilot period in Oldweigh, the author spent four days in the area office, with the different duty teams. She was able to sit in on interviews— with clients' permission—and go out on visits as well as study records. This period was used to develop the interview schedule that was to be tried out in the study. Pilot interviews were carried out with 20 families by the author and the research interviewer (a qualified social worker who knew the area, Patricia Wilkinson).

The research in the area team in Newpath was carried out by the author and an interviewer who was also a qualified social worker (Sally Thorpe).

The samples consisted of unselected referrals of households containing children under 14. A referral was defined as a contact with the relevant day's duty team by phone, face-to-face or letter, concerning a 'family unit' (at least one person over 18 and at least one under 14) that was not already an open case and that had an address in the area. Automatic notifications (for example, of juveniles by the police and of disconnections by the fuel boards) that were handled by an administrative process were not included in the referral sample unless they led to a contact (as previously defined) through the duty system.

One hundred referrals in Oldweigh were identified by the author, who attended the area office on 25 days and identified consecutive cases which met the research criteria. The duty team listed every contact in the duty book and entered details on a standard referral form. The preliminary observation period had shown that all contacts of cases not already open did in fact result in a referral form. The researcher noted details of the index referral and of the previous history from the referral form and from previous records.

The same procedures for identifying referrals that met research criteria were adopted in Newpath, where they were carried out by the interviewer (Sally Thorpe) after initial training. She identified 105 referrals on 25 days.

Only three referrals came from postcode areas outside the four sampled for the community survey in Newpath.

In 21 of the 100 identified cases in Oldweigh, and 23 of the 105 in Newpath, the referral did not lead to any direct contact with the family, who remained unaware of it. The majority of these families were the responsibility of another agency, and the referral merely involved the exchange of information. These cases were excluded from the survey. The 79 cases in Oldweigh and the 82 in Newpath who became aware of the referral formed the interview sample. There were no differences in household composition or previous social services contact between them and the excluded cases.

A letter explaining the research and inviting the parents to take part in an interview went out the day after the referral contact to all parents who were aware of the referral.

The interviewer visited the family as soon as possible after they had received the letter. The interview was carried out with the parent (or parent figure) who claimed most responsibility for the day-to-day care of the children. This person was identified by the interviewer at the beginning of her visit. The interview normally lasted for 45 minutes and was taped in a proportion of cases if the informant had no objection.

Table 6i shows how many were successfully interviewed and the reasons for failure. Seventy-two parents in each area agreed to take part (89 per cent of those eligible). Missing cases did not differ significantly on any of the variable available for comparison—age, sex, marital status, households composition, reason for referral.

Table 6i
Interview Sample: Reasons for Missing Cases

	Oldweigh	Newpath
Interviewed	72(91)	72(88)
Refused	4(5)	7(8)
No Trace	1(1)	3(4)
Excluded by Social Services	2(3)	—
All	79(100)	82(100)

1 partial interview in Oldweigh. Percentages in brackets.

The Interview Schedule

The schedule was developed to gather information on factors which previous research and the pilot work suggested were relevant to the generation and resolution of family problems. The evidence from previous research (Packman *et al.*, 1986; Creighton, 1985) suggested that families experiencing serious childrearing problems were distinguishable from the general run of families along a number of dimensions. These were notably:

• social disadvantage;

• previous family history indicating vulnerability;

• the nature of available informal social support;

Operational indicators were used to measure these three dimensions of family need.

Measures of current family problems were also included in the Interview Schedule:

• range and severity of current family problems;

• parental distress.

These various measures will now be described in more detail.

Social Disadvantage

A composite index of social disadvantage was developed incorporating indicators found to correlate with deprivation in other research (DHSS 1977; Essen & Wedge, 1982). They were:

Large family size   —5 + children under 16
3 + children under 5

Tenure category   —Not owner-occupier, council tenant or renting unfurnished

Overcrowding   —More than 1 person per room
More than 1.5 person per room

Lacks basic amenity
Lacks   —TV
Fridge
Washing-machine
Car

No wage-earner in household

A family scored one point for each indicator present. Thus a score of 11 indicated a family with maximum social disadvantage, and of 0 a family with no indicators of disadvantage. Families with scores of three or more were categorised as 'high' on social disadvantage; those with scores of two or less were categorised as 'low'.

Reliability of Disadvantage Index

The measures of social disadvantage were repeated at the follow-up interview, four months after the referral interview, so that the stability and reliability of the index could be examined. Most of the items making up the index remained much the same in both the research areas between the first and second interviews. Between 87 per cent and 99 per cent of families in both areas scored the same on 10 of the items in the index. Economic activity was the only item to show substantial changes: 13 per cent of households gained a wage-earner, and five per cent lost their wage-earner in Oldweigh; in Newpath 18 per cent of households gained a wage-earner during the four months follow-up, and only two per cent lost their wage-earner. However, the categorisation of cases into 'high' and 'low' on disadvantage was little affected. Over 90 per cent were in the same social disadvantage category at referral and four months later, giving a reasonable degree of stability to the index over this period.

Vulnerability

Various characteristics have been found in research studies which apparently distinguish families with serious problems (Jones, 1982). Because we were worried about risking our rapport with interviewed parents if we questioned them too closely about episodes in the past that might have appeared discreditable, we decided to use social services records as the main source for these sensitive data. This limited the number of variables we were able to include (and also restricted the measure of Vulnerability to the Referral Samples only). Pilot work showed, for example, that it would not be possible to use the records as reliable sources of information about previous drinking problems or psychiatric treatment. The following variables were included in a composite index of family vulnerability:

- mother under 20 at first birth;

- cohabiting adults, not joint parents;

- three or more house moves in last five years;

- child in household ever on register or case conference ever held or investigation for abuse/neglect;

- reported violence to a parent;

- reported criminal record of a parent.

A point was awarded for each item present, except child on register, which was awarded two. Thus the maximum attainable score was seven. As much of the data had to be obtained from social services records which were not always complete and were very difficult to use, these scores represent no more than crude estimates. Families with scores of two or more were regarded as 'high' on Vulnerability.

Indicators of this type are not to be regarded as *predictors* of problems such as child abuse or neglect, but rather as markers of family vulnerability and hence possible indicators of the need for help.

Social Support
To measure families' access to sources of social support and the degree to which they were socially isolated, an emended version of the Arizona Social Support Interview Schedule (ASSIS) was used. Network members are identified through a series of questions that probe for the names of individuals who provide defined categories of social support (Barrera, 1981 & 1985). The ASSIS provides measures such as the total number of supporters and those in conflict; the number giving different types of support; and the informant's satisfaction with support. It does not provide measures of the structure of the network itself.

Parental Distress
The Malaise Inventory was used as an indicator of the degree of depression and emotional distress being experienced by the parents. This is a 24-item questionnaire, adapted by Rutter and Graham from the Cornell Medical Inventory for use in a British community setting. The questions concern emotional and some physical symptoms and must be answered 'yes' or 'no'. A point is awarded for each positive response. The Malaise Inventory has been used as a measure of distress in many studies of parents, and its validity has recently been strongly maintained (Bebbington & Quine, 1986). In the original study on the Isle of Wight, scores of seven or more were considered critical—marking some sort of cut-off between the normal range of reactions and reactions that might be regarded as evidence of clinical disturbance (Rutter *et al.*, 1970).

Current Family Problems
During the pilot period a questionnaire was developed that contained 39 statements about a variety of family problems that parents coming to

social services frequently mentioned in the referral interviews we had observed. Parents were asked to agree or disagree (on Likert type of scale from strongly agree to strongly disagree) with each statement. Pilot interviews suggested that parents preferred a structured checklist of this kind to more discursive, open-ended questions. They could indicate the range of problems without having to give further details, unless they chose to do so. Factor analysis by a consultant (Professor B. T. Everitt) revealed five major dimensions in the data, and family problem scales were constructed accordingly. These were:

- Social contact;

- Parent-child problems (Parenting);

- Health;

- Finances;

- Marital problems (applying to the married or cohabiting).

Further discussion of the Family Problem Questionnaire is contained in Appendix 2.

Priority Groupings
Cluster analysis (Everitt, 1980) was used to classify the Samples into Priority Groups, using measures of needs and problems present at referral. Clustering techniques are particularly suitable in the exploration of complex multivariate data. The groups or clusters found may provide a useful summary of the data and suggest further hypotheses. The main purpose of using these techniques in the present study was to identify groups most in need of social services help. The particular method adopted by the consultant was the application of the k-means clustering algorithm. Solutions for two, three and four groups were reported. The three-group solution was selected for the referral samples as yielding the most meaningful clusters.

In the referral samples, the High Need group had high scores on measures of social disadvantage, parental Malaise and family problems. The Material Need group had high disadvantage and financial problems. The Coping group had fairly high disadvantage but scored relatively low at the time of referral on other problem measures.

Follow-Up of the Referral Samples
Four months after their index referral to social services, parents were invited to take part in a follow-up interview, for which they had been previously prepared. The follow-up interview repeated the initial one,

with only one section altered—the third, which had investigated pathways to the department and expectations of help, and on this second visit explored how the informant viewed any help received from social services, and other sources of help used since the index referral.

Table 6ii
Follow-Up Interviews: Success Rates

	Oldweigh	Newpath
Re-interviewed	61(86)	61(85)
Refused	3(5)	9(12)
Moved Away	6(8)	2(3)
Died	1(1)	—
All	71(100)	72(100)

Rounded percentages in brackets

Sixty-one informants were successfully re-interviewed in each area. (Table 6ii). There were no differences between re-interviewed and missing cases in disadvantage or vulnerability levels, in malaise, or in scores on the Family Problem Questionnaire. However, missing cases tended to be older.

Help obtained from Social Services
The county's central research section in Oldweigh provided a computer listing of all contacts of the sample with the social services department in the four months after the index referral. The listing included subsequent referrals; legal events; allocations to a social worker; and any resources used (such as financial payments, fostering, aids). The listing was the source of data on the services actually provided by the department during the four months after the index referral, but it was also checked against information provided by parents in the follow-up interview. In Newpath computer-isation was less advanced, and the information on the services received during the follow-up period had to be manually abstracted from records.

Parents in the Community Sample were asked a series of questions about their contacts with statutory and voluntary agencies, and in particular with the seven new family projects.

Social Work Questionnaires
All the social work members of staff in both area teams were asked to fill in questionnaires which attempted to tap the priority they gave to preventative work and community activities in carrying out their duties, and also explored their attitudes to preventive family social work and to community social work. As well, those social workers who worked with members of the referral sample during the follow-up period filled in a Family Support Activities Questionnaire about their work.

CHAPTER 7

Community and Referred Families:
Circumstances, Problems and Support Systems

Family Circumstances and Problems

The families in the Newpath community sample were drawn from the same neighbourhoods as the Newpath referral sample and therefore shared a common environment. Were the families referred to social services much the same as other families living in similar small areas? Or did they have exceptional problems, even when compared with their neighbours?

1. Family Structure

Families in the referral samples were exceptional in composition. First, the person most responsible for day-to-day care of the children was much more likely to be a lone parent: about half the referred were lone parents, but only about one in eight of the community sample (Table 7i). The great majority of lone parents were divorced women in their late twenties and early thirties, not single women.

While over half the referred families in both social services areas were headed by divorced or separated parents, reconstituted families—containing children who were not the offspring of both partners jointly—did not appear to be over-represented. Social services were attracting the divorced women who had not (or not yet) found another partner.

Table 7i
Lone Parenthood in Community and Referred Samples

Parent Status	Newpath		Oldweigh
	C	R	R
Lone Single	9(2)	9(12)	11(15)
Lone Divorced	38(11)	28(39)	25(35)
Married/Cohabiting	312(87)	35(49)	36(50)
All	359(100)	72(100)	72(100)

Percentages in brackets

Second, the households of referred families contained more children. The mean number of children in Newpath community sample was 1.97, compared to 2.51 and 2.73 in Newpath and Oldweigh Referral samples.

2. Social Disadvantage

The indicators of social disadvantage used in the study were explained in Chapter 6. Table 7ii compares the community and referral sample on the seven indicators. Since the samples were so different in family composition, lone parents and couples are shown separately.

Table 7ii
Indicators of Social Disadvantage in Community and Referred Samples

Disadvantage Indicators	Lone			Couples		
	Newp. Comm. (47)	Newp. Ref. (37)	Oldw. Ref. (36)	Newp. Comm. (312)	Newp. Ref. (35)	Oldw. Ref. (35)
% 5+ Children under 16	0	8	6	1	3	9
% 3+ Children under 5	0	5	6	2	9	14
% Temporary housing[1]	6	5	25	2	9	6
% 1+ per room	32	40	45	55	77	40
% 1.5+ per room	2	8	8	3	14	14
% Lacking Basič Amenity	4	3	17	<1	9	9
Mean Consumer Goods Lacking[2]	0.9	2.9	2.6	0.3	2.8	3.3
% No Wage-Earner	51	81	86	6	54	51
Mean Disadvantage Index	1.8	2.7	3.2**	0.9	3.0	2.3****

1. Bed & breakfast, hostel, etc.
2. Mean lacking of: car, TV, washing machine, refrigerator. Oneway Analysis of Variance: Disadvantage Index ** P < .01 Community v Oldweigh; **** P < .0001 Community v both Referred

The extent of disadvantage among referred couples in both samples was significantly greater than among the community couples. For example, over half the referred couples in both areas contained no wage-earner: only six per cent of couples in the community sample had no wage-earner. Referred lone parents were also more disadvantaged than community lone parents, but the difference was less marked.

Altogether, less than 10 per cent of referral families had no disadvantage indicators, while 32 per cent of community families had none. Nearly half the referred in both areas had three or more indicators of disadvantage, compared to only eight per cent of the community families.

Social class was difficult to determine because of the high proportion of women heads of household who were not working. An estimate, based on the Registrar General's classificatory system, was made on the basis of the man's present or last job for two-parent families, and the woman's last job for lone parents. On this definition, 52 per cent in Oldweigh referral sample were from semi or unskilled manual working-class backgrounds, compared with 38 per cent in Newpath referral and 25 per cent in Newpath community samples.

3. Attitudes to Housing and Neighbourhood

Parents were asked a series of questions about their own views of their housing and immediate neighbourhood. The results are summarised in Table 7iii.

Table 7iii
Satisfaction with Housing and Neighbourhood

	Newpath		Oldweigh	Sig.
	C	R	R	
	% Positive			
Enough Room in House	75	69	49	R v R*
				C v R NS
Enough Safe Play Space	89	68	49	R v R*
				C v R***
Satisfied with Housing	48	15	21	R v R NS
				C v R***
Would Like to Move	46	68	72	R v R NS
				C v R
Good Area to Bring up Children	59	40	31	R v R NS
				C v R*
Friendly Neighbourhood	41	28	29	R v R NS
				C v R***
Base Number	359	72	72	

Chi square statistics: * P < .05; ** P < .01; *** P < .001

Referred families in Newpath felt more satisfied with the roominess of their houses and their access to safe play space. Otherwise, there were no differences in attitude between the two referral samples, but there were marked differences between referred and community families. Referred parents were less satisfied with play space and with housing. They more often wanted to move. They less often felt their neighbourhood was a good one in which to bring up children, and they less often described the neighbourhood as definitely a friendly one. Thus referred families appeared to be less happily integrated into their nieghbourhoods.

Referred families were significantly more mobile than community families in similar areas. Referred parents in Newpath had made a mean 2.1 moves in the last five years, twice as many as the community parents. Thirty-seven per cent of referred parents had lived at their address for less than a year, compared to 17 per cent of community parents.

4. Family Problems

Referral and community families were compared in terms of two measures of current family problems, described in Chapter 6, the Family Problem Questionnaire and the Malaise Inventory. The first provided scores for four problem areas concerned with lack of social contact; parent-child difficulties; financial problems; and family members' ill-health. An additional problem area for the married or cohabiting only concerned difficult relationships with the partner.

Since the Family Problem Questionnaire was developed for this study, it should not be seen as a validated instrument. However, scores on the scales did relate to duty officers' categorisation of the client's main problem: parents whose main problem was described by the duty officer as concerned with child abuse or neglect scored significantly higher on the Parent-Child scale. Parents whose main problem, according to the duty officer, was financial, scored significantly higher on the Finances scale (Table 7iv).

Table 7iv
Family Problem Scales and Duty Officers' Descriptions of Main Problem

Main Referral Problem	Parent-Child Scale	Finances Scale
	Mean Score	
Abuse/Neglect (23)	24.9***	17.0
Non-Financial (44)	20.9	15.8
Financial (75)	18.7	19.5**

Numbers in brackets. 2 cases omitted for missing data.
Oneway Analysis of Variance: ** Finances v Non-F. $P < .01$; *** Abuse v Finances $P < .001$

Referred parents, living with or without a partner, had many more family problems of all types than did the community parents. As expected from the findings on social disadvantage, they had significantly higher scores on the Finances Scale. But they also reported significantly more parent-child difficulties, family health problems, marital problems and problems maintaining satisfactory social contacts.

5. Parental Malaise

The Malaise Inventory was used as an indicator of the emotional distress experienced by the parent who was chiefly responsible for the day-to-day care of the children. A parent overwhelmed with unpleasant feelings of anxiety and depression is likely to be less able to cope with the ordinary stresses and strains of parenthood, let alone with the serious problems that afflicted the referral samples.

There were no significant differences between the malaise scores of the two referral samples. In Newpath, there were highly significant differences between referred and community parents, whether lone (a mean score of 9.3 compared to 4.7) or couples (6.6 compared to 3.8). Fifty-one per cent of Newpath (and 68 per cent Oldweigh) referred parents had a score of seven or more on the Malaise Inventory, compared to only 21 per cent of the community parents. Referred parents appeared to be struggling with a much greater burden of anxious and depressed feelings than 'ordinary' families with similar aged children.

Table 7v summarises the correlations between scores on the Family Problem scales and on the Malaise Inventory. Each of the five scales was significantly positively correlated with malaise. Regression analysis indicated that the Family Problem scales were all independently related to malaise. The Parent-Child scale made the largest contribution. The Family Problem scales together explained half the variance in malaise (Multiple R .715 Adjusted R square .507).

Table 7v
The Relationship of Malaise Inventory Scores to Family Problem Scales

	Community (358)	Referred (138)
Parent-Child	.44**	.54**
Social Contact	.48**	.44**
Health	.35**	.44**
Money	.37**	.25*
Marriage	.33**	.39**

1 community and 6 referred cases excluded for missing data Correlations: * P < .01 ; ** P < .001

High-Need Groups

So far, the analysis has been concerned with scores on separate measures rather than with the needs, taken as a whole, of individual families. Scores on the various measures were used to pick out families, in both community and referral samples, who appeared to be most severely burdened with problems. Chapter 6 gave an account of the clustering method used. Eight variables were used in a separate analysis of lone parents and couples: age of main carer, disadvantage index, malaise score and scores on the Family Problem Questionnaire.

In the referral samples, a three group solution appeared the most meaningful. In Group 1 (27 per cent of the referrals) were parents who scored high on measures of disadvantage and financial problems and who also had high malaise scores and many non-financial family problems. Group 2 (36 per cent) contained younger parents who had equally serious disadvantage and financial difficulties, but lower malaise and other family problems. Group 3 (37 per cent) contained parents with somewhat lower mean disadvantage scores and generally lower levels of family problem. Thus families in Group 1 could be described as 'High Need'; Group 2 as 'Material Need'; and Group 3 as 'Coping'.

Because of the lower levels of disadvantage and problem scores in the community sample, a three group solution was not particularly meaningful. The two group solution was preferred. Group 1 contained 30 per cent of the community parents. They had higher needs, notably higher malaise scores, though they did not approach the problem levels of the referral sample. The remaining 70 per cent of community parents had low scores on all measures of needs.

In summary, the families referred to social services in the two areas of the study resembled each other closely in structure and in problem levels. However, families who had been randomly selected from similar neighbourhoods were strikingly different. Referred families were more often headed by lone parents. They had more indicators of social disadvantage and experienced more financial problems. They appeared less integrated into their neighbourhoods. They had more serious non-financial family problems and the main parent was more likely to be emotionally distressed.

Support Systems

For the purposes of this study, a supporter was considered to be someone who, in the words of Gerald Caplan, 'help(s) the individual mobilise his psychological resources and master his emotional burdens'. Supporters are people who provide 'supplies of money, materials, tools, skills and cognitive guidance' to improve the individual's handling of his situation (Caplan, 1974). Following Gottlieb (1983), the people who provide these kinds of help may be described, metaphorically, as an individual's 'support system'.

It has been suggested that a reason for referral to formal agencies, such as social services departments, may lie in the breakdown of informal support systems. If this were so, we should expect to find differences between the support systems of the referred and the community parents. To test this, community parents and referred parents were asked the same series of questions in order to identify the people to whom they turned for different kinds of help and support (see Chapter 6). The support systems were considered in terms of: types of support; types of provider; and degree of conflict.

The types of support investigated were:

- *Instrumental*
    * financial or material gifts or loans;

    * practical help with childcare;

    * practical help in the house, transport etc.

- *Emotional*
  * confiding private thoughts/feelings;
  * positive feedback, praise, thanks;
  * advice.

- *Social*
  * going out or having a good time in company.

  The types of provider were:

- *Relatives*
  * sexual partners;
  * sons and daughters;
  * mothers and fathers;
  * brothers and sisters;
  * parents-in-law and other in-law relations;
  * other relatives.

- *Informal*
  * friends;
  * neighbours (defined by propinquity);
  * other non-professionals, including ex-partners.

- *Professional*
  * doctors, health visitors, social workers, teachers, solicitors etc.

Parents identified specific people to whom they could turn for help of these various kinds. Parents were also asked to identify people with whom they expected to have an unpleasant disagreement which would make them angry or upset. These could be the same people already mentioned as supporters or different people.

Total Supporters
The first step was to examine all supporters named by the referred and the community parents in Newpath. Were the same types of people represented in similar proportions? Were people in the referred parents' networks more likely to be perceived as sources of conflict?

Friends made up the largest category (26 per cent of community members and 23 per cent of referral members). Then came non-first-degree relatives (17 per cent versus 14 per cent); parents (15 per cent versus 13

per cent); siblings (12 per cent versus 11 per cent); and sexual partners
(12 per cent versus nine per cent). Neighbours formed a small proportion
(three per cent versus four per cent). Professionals were more likely to
figure as referred parents' supporters (forming seven per cent as opposed
to four per cent of the membership), and so were children (11 per cent
versus seven per cent).

Table 7vi shows the proportion of all the people named who were
identified as likely to be the source of an unpleasant interaction. The first
column shows the proportion who were named both as giving one or
more types of support, and as sources of conflict. The second column
shows the proportion who were named only as sources of conflict.

Table 7vi
Types of Supporter in Newpath Community and Referred Samples:
Proportion in Conflicted Relationships

Type of Supporter	Community			Referred		
	Conflicted Support	Conflict Only	Total N	Conflicted Support	Conflict Only	Total N
	% of Total			% of Total		
Sexual Partner	19	3	313	32	6	47
Child	15	8	182	32	20	69
Parent	1	4	400	14	9	76
Sibling	3	5	312	5	11	63
Other Relative	6	6	454	5	5	75
Friend	2	1	673	2	2	118
Neighbour	3	27	111	0	26	27
Other Lay	3	25	133	2	18	51
Professional	0	4	112	2	7	40*

Neighbours most often figured as sources of conflict, in the community
as well as the referred systems (30 per cent versus 26 per cent of all
neighbours named were sources of conflict). Sexual partners and children
were also likely to provide conflicts—but much more often in the
referred systems. Nearly twice as many sexual partners, and over twice as
many children, figured as sources of conflict in the referred networks. The
same trend was seen for parents and siblings.

Individual Support Systems

Contrary to expectation, referred and community parents identified similar
numbers of instrumental, emotional and social supporters (Table 7vii). In
general, couples, whether community or referred, had more supporters.

Table 7vii
Support and Conflict: Community and Referred Parents

Types of Support	Lone				Couples			
	Newp. Comm. (47)	Newp. Ref. (37)	Oldw. Ref. (36)		Newp. Comm. (310)	Newp. Ref. (35)	Oldw. Ref. (35)	
				Mean Supporters				
Instrumental	3.98	3.81	3.50	NS	4.17	5.06	4.51	<.10
Emotional	3.91	3.76	3.92	NS	3.67	3.97	4.11	NS
Social	1.94	1.84	1.28	NS	2.61	1.91	2.69	NS
Conflicted	1.21	1.46	1.86	<.10	0.85	1.83	1.94	****

2 Community and 1 Referred case omitted for missing data
Oneway Analysis of Variance: **** P < .0001 Community v Oldweigh Referred

There were differences in the types of supporter named. Referred parents more often named friends, and less often named close family members, especially as instrumental supporters. This was not due to any difference in actual availability of relatives: similar numbers had been seen by referred and community parents in the previous month.

Referred parents were significantly more likely to name people with whom they expected to have unpleasant encounters (conflicted relationships). The difference was most striking for couples: .85 mean conflicted relationships in Newpath community sample; 1.83 in Newpath referral sample; and 1.94 in Oldweigh referral sample. Excess conflicts with partners and children largely accounted for these differences.

Satisfaction with Support

Two qualitative measures were also used in assessing the parents' support systems. Informants were asked to use 3-point scales (for each of the seven categories of support) to rate their satisfaction with support, and how much they needed that support during the previous month. A summary measure of 'support satisfaction' was then obtained by counting the number of categories (out of seven) where the informant was satisfied: a score of 0 implied complete dissatisfaction with support, while one of seven represented maximum satisfaction. A summary measure of 'support need' was obtained by counting the number of categories where the informant expressed a need for 'quite a bit' of support.

Support need and support satisfaction were inversely correlated, in both referred and community samples. The more need parents felt for support, the less satisfied they were likely to be (r $-$.36). Referred parents—lone and couples—expressed significantly more needs for support and less satisfaction with it (Table 7viii).

Table 7viii
Needs for and Satisfaction with Support: Community and Referred Parents

Support	Lone				Couples			
	Newp. Comm. (46)	Newp. Ref. (37)	Oldw. Ref. (36)		Newp. Comm. (312)	Newp. Ref. (35)	Oldw. Ref. (35)	
				Means				
Needs Index	1.4	3.5	3.6	****	0.8	2.3	2.9	****
Satisfaction Index	5.7	3.9	3.6	****	6.0	4.8	3.5	****

1 Community and 1 Referred Case omitted for missing data
Oneway Analysis of Variance: **** P < .0001 Community v Referred Samples

For both referred and community parents, the actual number of *conflicted* relationships had a significant relationship to support need and support satisfaction. The more conflicted relationships, the higher the need for support, and the less satisfaction with it. Among the referred parents, satisfaction with support was positively related to the number of *instrumental* supporters: parents who named more people who gave help with money, childcare or other practical help were more satisfied overall with their support. Among the community parents, satisfaction with support was not correlated with the number of supporters.

In summary, there was little difference in the *quantity* of support available to referred and community parents. The main difference was in the sources of support and in its quality. Referred parents relied more on friends and professionals and less on close family members, especially for instrumental support. They expressed more need for, and less subjective satisfaction with, their support.

Conflict with others emerged as a key factor. Referred parents were significantly more likely to nominate close family members as people with whom they expected to conflict, but they were no more likely to expect conflict with neighbours, friends or more distantly related family. Conflict, therefore, appeared to characterise their more intimate relationships rather than their social relationships in general.

Support and Malaise
Was there any evidence that the amount or type of support had any bearing on parents' capacity to cope with problems? It has already been demonstrated that people with many family problems also had high malaise scores. If support acted as a buffer against stress, it might be expected that high scorers on the Family Problem Questionnaire, who also had large support systems, would have some protection against

emotional distress: they should have lower malaise scores than high Family Problem scorers with smaller support systems. The data shown in Table 7ix suggest that this was indeed the case for instrumental support. Parents with many family problems and six or more instrumental supporters had a mean malaise score of 6.7, compared to 9.5 for parents with many problems but less than three instrumental supporters.

Table 7ix
Malaise, Family Problems and Number of Instrumental Supporters

Number of Instrumental Supporters	Family Problems	
	High	Low
	Mean Malaise Score	
0–2	9.50(56)	3.29(72)
3–5	8.39(102)	2.94(135)
6+	6.70(50)	2.78(81)

Combined samples: Numbers in brackets. Data missing on 6 cases

Two way Analysis of Variance	Sum of Squares	DF	F	Signif
Main Effects	3528.02	3	86.66	.000
Family Problems	3330.59	1	245.44	.000
Instrumental Support	134.18	2	4.94	.007
2-way Interactions Family Problems/Support	85.786	2	3.16	.04
Explained	3613.81	5	53.26	.000
Residual	6649.21	490		
Multiple Classification Analysis				
Multiple R squared	.344			
Multiple R	.586			

The presence of conflicted relationships also appeared to influence malaise, independently of the level of family problems. There were signs of an interaction effect, with conflict appearing to have more influence when there were many family problems (Table 7x).

It could be argued then, taking the three samples together, that the availability of people to give practical help with money, childcare and other domestic tasks appeared to be important in reducing personal stress caused by high levels of family problems. Emotional and social support appeared less effective, when measured as here in quantitative terms.

Table 7x
Malaise, Family Problems and Conflicted Relationships

Conflicted Relationships	Family Problems	
	High	Low
	Mean Malaise Score	
None	5.90(30)	2.70(136)
One or More	7.95(92)	3.19(117)

Numbers in brackets. 7 cases omitted with missing data

Analysis of Variance	Sum of Squares	DF	F	Signif
Main Effects	1749.367	2	84.29	.000
Family Problems	1377.37	1	132.73	.000
Conflicted Relationships	69.45	1	6.69	.01
2-way Interactions				
Family Problems/Conflict	40.29	1	3.88	.05
Explained	1789.66	3		
Residual	3849.93	371		
Multiple R squared	.310			
Multiple R	.557			

Conflict with others appeared to make problems harder to tolerate, in that parents with many family problems who were also in conflict with others endured more malaise. Since referred parents were caught up in more conflict (as well as having more family problems) they were at a double disadvantage in comparison with the community parents.

CHAPTER 8

Use of Organised Supportive Services

The Community Families: Contact with Services

The last chapter described parents' personal support. This one will examine their use of organised services. The results from the community survey will first be used to give an overall picture of parents' contact with local services. Then, their use of the innovative family projects will be examined in more detail. Lastly, the referred families' experiences of the social services departments will be described.

What use did ordinary families make of local services? Table 8i sets out the complete picture of service use by the Newpath community sample in the 12 months before interview. Health-based services (general practitioners and health visitors) were by far the most likely to be contacted. Over 90 per cent of families had been in touch with a GP and nearly half with a health visitor in the previous year. Playgroups had been used by 58 per cent of families with under-fives. A third had contacted Social Security services (a seemingly high proportion, probably reflecting the nature of the areas we surveyed). Police and legal services were also heavily used, by over a quarter. About as many had contacted the Citizens Advice Bureau as had contacted a social worker (12 to 13 per cent). The remaining services were used by less than 10 per cent of the sample.

Social Services Department

At first sight, knowledge of the social services department among ordinary parents appeared to be widespread. Three hundred and forty people (95 per cent of the sample) said they had heard of it. However, only 118 (33 per cent) could name the address of the area office correctly or approximately. Many people (nearly 40 per cent) had only a vague idea of how they had come to hear about the social services department, or said they had 'always known' of it. Friends and acquaintances were the most common sources of information for the remainder (19 per cent of all those who had heard of the department), followed by news media (14 per cent), relatives (nine per cent) and work (eight per cent).

Table 8i
Contact with Community Services in Previous Year

	Total Families	Families with Children Under 5
General Practitioner	339(94)	225(97)
Health Visitor	170(47)	165(71)
Play/Mother & Toddler Group	152(42)	134(58)
Social Security	120(33)	89(38)
Solicitor/Other Legal	82(28)	NK
Police	81(23)	44(19)
Citizens Advice Bureau	46(13)	32(14)
Social Services/Other Social Worker	45(12)	30(13)
Nursery School	42(12)	37(16)
Vicar/Priest	24(7)	NK
Neighbourhood Family Project*	16(4)	12(5)
Child Minder	12(3)	10(4)
Day Nursery	8(2)	7(3)
Gingerbread	7(2)	5(2)
NSPCC	4(1)	3(1)
Phone Help (Samaritans etc.)	* 4(1)	3(1)
Home-Start	3(1)	2(1)
Marriage Guidance (Relate)	3(1)	2(1)
Psychiatrist	1(<1)	NK
BASE NUMBER	359(100)	232(100)

* Any of four named locally based family projects.

Informants who had heard of the social services department were asked what they thought it did. Rather more than 40 per cent of those who had heard of the department gave answers that suggested they had a fairly clear idea of at least some of its functions. They knew the department was concerned with families (21 per cent), children (12 per cent), or the disabled and elderly (3 per cent). However, 16 per cent had no idea what the social services department did, and a sizeable proportion (43 per cent) gave answers that suggested they believed the department's main purpose was to provide financial help. Many of these seemed to think it was the same as Social Security (DHSS as it was usually known).

It assesses people for benefit payments and pays it out if necessary. They have a children's department looking out for children in need.

It helps you if you are unemployed or on low wages.

They help you with money if you are short.

They help families out when they need clothes, food and money.

Only eight people appeared overtly critical of the social services department, or saw it as interfering.

> They stick the nose in when they are not wanted. I just know from my friends they interfere when they are not needed.

Use of the Social Services Department

Altogether, 45 people (12.5 per cent of the sample) had been in contact with a social worker in the 12 months before the interview. Thirty-one of these said they had seen a social worker from the area office, while 14 more had seen one based elsewhere, such as in hospital or in child guidance. Lone parents, and families who fell into the High Need cluster described in the last chapter, were significantly more likely to have contacted a social worker. Thirty-two per cent of High Need lone parents had made contact compared with 18 per cent of High Need couples and nine per cent of Low Need couples. People who had used social services in the previous 12 months were asked structured questions about the kinds of help they had sought from the department, and whether they thought they had received such help.

The most frequent reason for seeking help from a social worker—especially one based in the area office as opposed to the hospital or clinic—was the need for welfare rights advice, financial or material help or advocacy—putting one's case to some other person or agency. Just over half those who had seen a social worker in the previous 12 months had done so for one or more of these reasons. The great majority said they had received some help of the kind they had sought. Some who had received this kind of practical help continued to betray confusion about the difference between the social services department and Social Security.

> I went to them through having my gas nearly cut off. Well the DHSS is the social services. I got the advice as to what to do not to have my gas cut off.

Only a few people had sought help from social workers for personal problems or problems with children, but over three-quarters of those who had, reported that they had received some help. For example, one mother had asked for her child to be assessed because he was truanting and had set fire to the bedroom, and he had been placed in a foster home for a while for this purpose. Similarly, the 12 people who reported seeking other kinds of help had nearly always managed to get it. For example, one woman had sought and obtained help and advice in relation to her mentally-ill mother.

We asked people what was the most useful help they had received as a result of their contact with the social services area team. Advice and moral support were most often spontaneously mentioned, followed by specific help with children. In summary, the evidence from the community survey suggested that ordinary people with no special knowledge still often found it hard to distinguish between the functions of the social services department and those of the Social Security system. Nearly everyone in the sample had heard of the social services department, but less than half had any clear idea of what its purpose might be. The department was most often seen as a source of advice and help in getting welfare benefits and other material help. It was not surprising, therefore, to find that the most common reason for contacting social workers—especially those based in the area office—during the 12 months before the interview was to obtain this kind of practical help. Many people needing financial advice and advocacy appeared to be turning to the department as if it were a general advice centre like the Citizens Advice Bureau, or believing it to be attached in some way to the Social Security system.

Contact with Family Projects
The new family projects in Newpath were described in chapter 5. We saw that the neighbourhood projects had open-door policies. Nevertheless they (and their funders) hoped to be of service to families with the greatest needs, as well as to other local families. What was unclear was the actual mix of users. If the projects attracted too many people in difficulties, would they become stigmatised and avoided by families in general? If they were used mainly by 'coping' families, would people with problems feel intimidated and stay away?

The first step was to establish how well the projects were actually known. Altogether, there were 211 replies indicating knowledge of a neighbourhood family project, and 100 indicating knowledge of Home-Start.

Friends, acquaintances and neighbours—'word of mouth' as some put it—were the most frequently cited sources of initial information about the projects. The local paper was the next best source of information: people remembered news items and advertisements. Quite a number had noticed the neighbourhood family projects just because they lived locally. Other sources of information were infrequently cited.

When asked what they thought the projects did, respondents sometimes appeared vague. Approaching a third of those who said they had heard of a Project were unable to name anything it did:

> Its just a name I've heard—that's all.
>
> I heard of it through a college course—but what they do I've no idea.
>
> Heard of it on the radio. Can't say what it does.

Others gave firm but confused answers. For example, eight per cent of respondents who had heard of Home-Start thought it was an organisation to help invalids or the elderly; and 15 per cent thought it was something to do with providing furniture or moving house.

Rather less than half the respondents who had heard of a project were able to give an approximately accurate description of what it did, as in the following examples:

It supports young parents in the home in practical ways, takes them shopping, gives friendship. (*Home-Start*)

They help children and one-parent families who can't cope, marriage guidance, social security advice, just someone to chat to. (*Herding*)

It gives advice about benefits. It has get-togethers for mums and babies, it looks after children so mums can have a chat. They also have volunteers for parents who are under stress. (*Newton*)

It helps young mums get together, keep fit, sale of second-hand clothes, a creche for schoolchildren in the school holidays. Oh all sorts of different things really for you to do. (*Ashgrove*)

Reasons for Lack of Contact

One hundred and forty-seven individual respondents (41 per cent) had heard of one or more Neighbourhood Family Projects. Of these, 30 had actually made contact. One hundred individuals had heard of Home-Start, of whom 10 had made contact. Why did people not make use of their knowledge to contact a project? One reason, as we have seen, was that many had only a vague idea of what the projects were for. Nearly a quarter gave 'distance' as their main reason for not making contact. For the remainder, easily the most common reason was that people perceived the projects as being for a certain kind of family—a problem family, or one that couldn't cope with its own difficulties. They did not see their own families in this light, and equally did not appear to consider themselves, in most cases, as possible helpers or volunteers. The replies did suggest that a certain degree of stigma attached to the projects:

They go round talking to parents who are depressed or lonely or need advice about their children. I don't need anything like that.

They are experienced mums who help at visiting problem families. They go round visiting mothers who need help. I have no need for help.

How People Contacted the Projects

Home-Start's policy was to recruit most of its clients through professionals. In our survey, six of the ten people who had contacted Home-Start attributed their first contact to a health visitor or social worker, and three more said they had been approached by the organiser without their having to take any initiative. By contrast, the points of entry to the

Neighbourhood Projects were more diverse, reflecting their open-door policies. Over a third said they had just popped in out of curiosity, or for a specific event.

> I just went there I think basically out of curiosity the first time. (*Ashgrove*)

> It's just across the road so I went to a Mother Toddler Group. (*Hilldon*)

> I heard they were doing a keep-fit course so I went in. (*Herding*)

Nearly a quarter said they needed help and approached the project on their own initiative.

> I was expecting my last baby and couldn't get any help with money from DHSS. A friend told me about them. (*Ashgrove*)

> I saw it in the Link magazine. I went because I wanted to talk to someone about my feelings of having a handicapped child. (*Newton*)

Expectations

We tried to explore the initial expectations of people who had contacted a project. In answer to our question whether they had initially approached the project in the hope of some kind of help, about half agreed that they had. The remainder had gone for a variety of other reasons, of which the most common was to socialise or for 'something to do'.

> I know the woman who runs it. I just want to meet people. Didn't want help. (*Herding*)

Only three respondents said they had initially gone because they wanted to help others in some way.

There was some difference between the family projects, with Home-Start attracting more people in search of counselling with personal problems or problems with children:

> I needed help with Julie. She can't go to a normal playgroup because of her illness. It was somewhere I could go where I had confidence they could cope, that they knew what they were doing. I had problems as well and it was a place where I could get some help. (*Home-Start*)

> I got in a state over my children when my marriage broke up. I needed someone to listen to me, just someone to talk to when I was feeling down. (*Home-Start*)

> When we moved I suffered serious depression. I was having trouble with my marriage and couldn't turn to my husband. It provides a friend, someone to talk to. (*Home-Start*)

About a third of those who contacted projects had sought information about services or benefits, or help with finances:

> They help on money matters, same sort of thing as a social worker. I just read it on a leaflet and when I was pregnant I went to ask them about what I could claim. (*Newton*)

Locality and Use

The four Neighbourhood Family Projects were intended to serve residents from their own neighbourhoods, and in fact individual projects were rarely used by outsiders. Two-thirds of local respondents knew of the Herding Centre, but the other projects were rather less well known in their areas. Three out of the four had been used by nine to ten per cent of the respondents from their own local areas in the last 12 months—a rather low proportion.

Family Needs and Use of Projects

One test of the success of the projects was the degree to which they were able to attract families with the greatest needs, as well as those with fewer needs. To what extent were the projects used by parents with the greatest social needs?

We first looked at the degree of contact achieved by the Neighbourhood Projects with socially disadvantaged families in their local areas, and found that they attracted significantly more of them—more than a quarter of the poorest families. In their own areas, the projects were achieving as much contact with these priority groups as was the social services area team—quite an achievement considering the different scale of their operations.

It is notable that, with the exception of Social Security, other services did *not* attract significantly higher proportions of people with the greatest needs. Playgroups, indeed, attracted significantly fewer of them: 71 per cent of parents of under-fives with least social disadvantage were using playgroups, compared to 46 per cent of the most socially disadvantaged parents.

The community sample was then divided into four groups: lone parents in the high and low need clusters (described in chapter 6), and couples in those clusters. Only four per cent of Low Need couples had ever contacted a family project, compared with 16 per cent of High Need couples. Lone-parent families had higher rates of contact regardless of Need Group. Over three quarters of High Need lone parents, however, who might be seen as the group with the highest priority of all, were not using the projects (Table 8ii).

Table 8ii
Contact with Family Projects: High and Low Need Groups

	Lone		Couple	
	Needs:			
	High	Low	High	Low
Family Projects				
Used	4(22)	10(33)	14(16)	10(4)
Not Used	15(79)	20(67)	75(84)	210(96)
ALL	19(100)	30(100)	89(100)	220(100)

Percentage in brackets. 1 case omitted for missing data.

Experiences of Those Who Contacted Family Projects
The experience of those who went to the family projects was naturally variable, reflecting their different expectations and needs. So that we could be sure of getting the same information about all five projects, we asked a series of structured questions about their activities and the users' evaluation of them. Since the numbers were small the results are presented for the combined projects. There were 38 individual users, who reported on 41 separate experiences with different projects.

In spite of the variability in the expectations and experiences of people who contacted the projects, some patterns could be discerned. There were only a few abortive contacts: people went to a project under a misapprehension, or made a fleeting connection which was not pursued because the time was not right.

Patterns of Use
There seemed to be three typical patterns among those who had more extended contact. **Consumers** did not see themselves as in need of any help, but wanted to take advantage of a facility on offer at a project. Consumers had not so far progressed on from this to any wider involvement in the organisation of the project itself (they answered 'no' to a question about whether they had helped in running things). Fourteen of the experiences with projects fell into this group.

> They have a thrift shop on a Friday where you can buy second-hand clothes cheap. I don't go for any other reason.
>
> I just go to the Mother and Toddlers group to meet friends, that's all.
>
> We have a child to stay through social services in the summer. I take him on their outings.

Clients were using a project—in rather the same way that they might have used a solicitor or social services—because they needed help. They obtained some service—whether counselling, advisory or practical—and were apparently content with the role of service recipient. Thirteen of the contacts fell into this group. Clients were often seeking welfare rights advice or practical help, though a few had sought help with more personal difficulties.

> I wanted to find out about my daughter, whether she was entitled to social and where we could go for help.

> I phoned up for an appointment and saw someone who gave me advice. That's all I wanted—advice about financial matters.

> I was trying to get a better job. My husband became unemployed so I needed to earn more.

> I had a letter through from the council about the garden. I went round to get help with doing the garden.

> I just needed someone to listen to me, just someone to talk to when I was feeling down. I didn't join in anything else. Just had someone to visit me and talk to me.

The last group, whom we will call **Members** of the projects were perhaps the most interesting. These were people who may have started out as Consumers or Clients but whose involvement with the project had taken on a broader character. They had become identified with it, to the point were they were prepared to play a more active part in its running and give up time to organisational activities. They saw themselves as helping others, as well as being helped, by their involvement. Eight of the experiences with projects had developed in this way.

> I just went there because a friend of mine went. It gets you involved in all sorts. I've just been doing some yoga and we've recently started doing Shiatsu. It's a form of Chinese massage. It sort of relaxes you when you're all tensed like me. You can practically do what you like there and it's been a godsend to me. I just wanted to get out of the house really and get away from him (invalid relative). It's somewhere to meet others, maybe in a similar position or worse even, to discuss your problems with and let fly, get things off your chest. (*Ashgrove*)

> The social worker put me onto it. The children have a playleader and loads of helpers—Toys, oranges and biscuits. Mothers can stay and talk, have coffee and biscuits. Every family has a helper allocated to them and they visit every other week. You can call them any time day or night. They give you advice, listen to your problems and find out how you can be helped if they don't know the answer. They are very supportive and gave me advice when I needed it. When daughter starts school I want to go on the course so I can become a helper. I'm going to ask the organiser about it. It's a very good organisation. (*Home-Start*)

Its an advice centre for rights, coffee morning, literary group, thrift shop, links new mums together. I wanted support when the baby was ill. I made new friends when I was new to the area, my ex-husband was arrested and they sorted it out. I've also contacted them for Gingerbread to distribute furniture. It's a very good place, very friendly, a useful part of the community. A nice place to drop into. (*Herding*)

The pattern of activities undertaken at the projects was different as between Consumers, Clients and Members (Table 8iii).

Table 8iii
Activities of Family Projects

Activity	Consumers	Clients	Members
	% Performing Activity		
Drop-In/Coffee Morning	43	23	75
Play Activity	43	8	62
Welfare Rights/Material Help	21	69	50
Sale/Exchange Clothes etc.	14	15	25
Crafts etc.	7	15	62
Trip/Holiday	29	15	62
Organisational	7	0	88
BASE NUMBER	14	13	8

Members took part in a greater spread of activities of all kinds. Clients were least involved, tending to use a project in answer to a specific need or problem, most often of a practical kind.

Benefits Gained by Users
We also asked respondents to tell us what had happened to them during their contact with the particular project. We hoped to tap into respondents' views of how they may have benefited from attendance (Table 8iv).

In summary, of the 41 identified contacts with family projects, only six proved abortive. Thirty-five of the contacts (85 per cent) resulted in some degree of participation and benefit. As we would expect, Members had gained more from their experiences with the projects than had Consumers or Clients. Having a good time and making new friends were gains experienced by at least some in all three groups, but Members were much more likely to grow in confidence and, probably as a result, to speak up in meetings and take part in decision-making. Overall, the most commonly experienced gains were in increased opportunities for social contact and having a good time. These positive social outcomes should not be underestimated, especially on estates where loneliness and isolation are common experiences for mothers with young children. By enlarging people's social circles in this way, the family projects may be helping to increase resilience and the ability to cope with stress. About a fifth of the contacts had resulted in a broader involvement with the project, enabling users to take on responsibility and acquire a range of new skills. This could not have been achieved through statutory services, whose users must remain in fixed client roles.

Table 8iv
What Users Gained From Attending Family Projects

Outcome	Consumers	Clients	Members
	% With Outcome		
Had a good time	57	23	100
Made new friends	36	23	88
Gained confidence	21	23	75
Had help with children	14	23	62
Helped others	14	23	88
Understood self better	0	31	62
Understood others better	7	31	75
Learned something new	7	15	75
Spoke up in meetings	7	0	50
Helped to run activities	0	0	100
Took part in decisions	0	0	62
Took on new responsibilities	7	0	50
BASE	14	13	8

Satisfaction With Formal Services and Family Projects

Table 8v summarises the satisfaction expressed by users of the family projects, and compares this with satisfaction ratings for selected statutory and voluntary services.

Table 8v
Satisfaction with Services: Users' Views

	Very Sat.	Fairly Sat.	Neutral	Fairly Dissat.	Very Dissat.
			% Users		
Play Group (112)	70	19	7	3	1
Health Visitor (170)	64	26	5	2	3
Citizens Advice Bureau (46)	63	24	4	7	2
General Practitioner (339)	62	27	5	5	1
Nursery School (42)	60	33	2	2	2
Family Projects (41)	49	24	22	5	0
Police (81)	46	27	8	10	9
Youth Club (20)	45	35	15	5	0
Mother and Toddler Group (71)	45	34	5	13	3
Social Services Area Team (31)	35	16	22	6	19
Social Security (120)	25	37	9	11	18

Base number of users in brackets

Of the statutory services, general practitioners and health visitors gave most satisfaction to their users, with around 90 per cent being fairly or very satisfied. Three-quarters of all users of the family projects were fairly or very satisfied—the same proportion as for the police. The social services department and Social Security aroused rather more dissatisfaction, but over half their users rated them positively. Satisfaction ratings for other services used by at least 20 people in the previous year are also shown. All were rated favourably, but playgroups stood out: 70 per cent of their users were very satisfied with them, an even better result than that achieved by the Citizens Advice Bureau. Mother and Toddler Groups, however, appeared somewhat less successful from their users' point of view.

The Contribution of the Family Projects

The survey was carried out on the estates where neighbourhood family projects had been established, so as to maximise our chances of interviewing users in the community. However, the Meadow Centre did not become operational as soon as we had hoped, so that about two-thirds of the sample lived in areas adjacent to an established Project. This reduced the number of users in the sample.

Results suggested that the family projects were not as well known as perhaps they should be. Three of the four neighbourhood family projects were known to less than half the interviewed families in their areas. The longest established (Herding), however, was better known, to two-thirds of local families in the survey. It probably takes a good many years for a project to make a name for itself in its neighbourhood.

The survey results suggested that in the course of a year the neighbourhood family projects might be contacted by about 10 per cent of the families (with under-14s) in their areas. They were reaching a larger proportion of the families with the greatest needs. Lone parents and families with many social needs and problems were significantly more likely to be users of a family project than were couples, and families with fewer social needs. In their ability to attract the disadvantaged, the family projects differed from other services which were more significant numerically. Playgroups, for example, which were much more widely used and were held in great favour by their users, appealed significantly more to the advantaged (relatively speaking).

The family projects, therefore, were making a greater contribution to families with the greatest needs. There was no evidence from our survey that users felt in any way stigmatised or ashamed of their contact with the projects. On the contrary, there was evidence that some at least were gaining in confidence and taking on new responsibilities as well as forming links with others. The projects' ability to bring people together and forge new friendships meant that they were strengthening users' personal support systems. If effective supportive networks enhance people's ability to withstand stress without developing physical and mental symptoms, family projects could be making an important contribution to public health.

However, just because of their success in attracting people with problems, the projects were generally seen as less relevant to most ordinary families, even when parents knew of them. Since they were seen as places for people with problems, those who saw themselves as coping adequately did not make contact. This mattered less for a project like Home-Start, which operated on a referral system and existed to help individual families under stress, than for the neighbourhood family projects which had broader aims. It may be difficult to combine the aims of helping families in difficulties and of becoming a force for community development, attractive to a much wider range of families.

Referred Families: Contact with Social Services

Why did the parents in the referral samples contact social services? Did the presence of more voluntary family support resources in Newpath mean that parents there were using statutory services in a different way from those in Oldweigh?

Under a quarter of cases in Oldweigh, and under a third in Newpath were new referrals, coming to the department for the first time. On average, families in both areas had had between three and four referrals over the previous five years, and over half the re-referrals had been last seen less than a year ago. While about a third in both areas had been previously allocated to a social worker's caseload, the most common pattern was of repeated duty contacts which never led to a more extended period of contact.

The researcher had expected that there would be some differences in the referral patterns of the two areas. Since there was an established network of locally based family projects in Newpath offering advice services, there should have been less need for parents there to approach social services for financial advice and advocacy. In fact there proved to be little difference between the areas. Only slightly fewer referred themselves in Newpath (53 per cent versus 61 per cent), and over half in both areas were classified by the social services duty officer as having a financial or housing problem as the main reason for contact. People who referred themselves were most likely to be classed as having financial problems. The most common reason for referral by others was suspicion of child abuse or neglect.

Parents' Expectations of Social Services

During the first research interview, parents themselves described why they had sought help (or been referred) to social services. The researchers recorded their replies verbatim and classified them, using the same method as for the social workers' accounts of referral problems.

Financial Problems

The largest group of parents (55 per cent in Oldweigh and 61 per cent in Newpath) said that their main reason for contacting the department had been a financial or material problem.

> We didn't have no food to feed our kids at all. We were desperate for enough money to tide us over until we get our next giro. (347)

> Needed help towards paying for playschool for Jim. I thought they would send a form through the post but they have to come out and interview. Knowing my luck I won't get it anyway. (359)

> I was having problems with social security about making claims while my husband was in hospital. One minute DHSS told me to claim and then they said he had to make the claim. I had to get forms from him saying I could claim on his behalf but I hadn't the money to go to the hospital. I hoped social services would give me advice on what to do. (308)

> I had no money and DHSS was refusing to make a payment because I lost my purse. I wanted advice if that was correct. (52)

The duty social workers in both areas agreed on the client's perception of the main problem as a financial or housing one in 69 out of 82 possible cases (84 per cent agreement). Social workers did not seem to look for underlying reasons for these material difficulties (as they are alleged to do by some), but largely recorded the client's presentation without comment.

Family Relationships

Twenty-four parents described their main reason for contacting social services as being the wish for some help with a child's difficult behaviour, or with some other family relationship problem.

> Tom wouldn't go to school. I was threatened with legal action—£400 fine or a month in prison. I couldn't pay or go to prison because I've got Judy to look after. I phoned social services three times—Hoped they would talk to Tom and help him sort out his problem out at school. A couple of teachers keep picking on him. (3)

> I can't control the kids—can't see what I'm doing wrong. Kids are cheeky, they won't do as they're told unless shouted at. They're rude, crude, they swear. One child was sent home at lunchtime because he hit the headmaster.

One is stealing from me and the other children. I need someone to find out what is wrong with the kids. (63)

We're finding my son lies to the bus driver—told him to drop him off at the shop. I spanked him. We don't know if it's because he hasn't seen his dad for four weeks. I wanted social services help to see if we could get to the bottom of why he had done this. (307)

There was rather less agreement between social workers' and clients' perceptions of this type of problem: in 14 out of the 24 cases, social workers saw the problem in the same way as the parents. Where there was disagreement, the social workers tended to lay more stress on parents' inappropriate methods of discipline or care, rather than to accept the parents' point of view that the children were out of control. The social workers sometimes saw risk to the child where the parents had tried to describe a child whose behaviour was beyond them. For example, one mother 'felt suicidal' because her son, who had previously been in trouble with the police and in voluntary care, had now broken into his father's safe and was quite beyond their control. The social worker laid more stress on father's having hit the boy and 'drawn blood from his mouth' and on mother's also having hit him.

Risk to Children

Parents themselves described concerns about a child's safety or adequate care as the main referral problem in only 12 cases:

Social workers just turned up on the doorstep. I had no idea they were coming. The person I was living with at the time had a record of child violence. They threatened to remove my daughter unless I told my boyfriend to leave. I hoped they would listen and continue to visit regularly to check everything was OK. Then I could have gone on living with him. (31)

My daughter was indecently assaulted by my neighbour and father-in-law. I was told to keep it secret from my husband but he found out through his father and they said I had fabricated the whole story. I had to leave as I was frightened for myself and my daughter. I talked to the health visitor and she rang social services. A social worker came here, then they said that as child guidance was involved that would solve my problems. (352)

Social workers perceived situations where a child was 'at risk' twice as often as parents did. However, they tended to see violence to a woman as specific and not also involving risk to a child, whereas mothers in this position took a different view. For example, one young mother whose husband had a serious drinking problem described his violence to her and that she had eventually made up her mind to seek help because she was worried he might do something to the baby. She hoped the social worker would speak to her husband or, if that failed, find her alternative accommodation because her name was not on the rent book. However, the social worker saw the situation as involving marital violence only. There was nothing the department could do since there had been no violence to the baby. He therefore advised her to consult the housing department and seek legal advice.

Financial problems were often of very recent onset—emergencies that had arisen in the last week. The majority of other problems had lasted for over a month, and the majority of problems over a child's difficult behaviour had lasted for over a year.

Since most of the referrals had been known to social services for some years, it was not surprising that when we tried to explore the pathways by which parents had reached the department on this occasion we found that the majority had apparently turned to the department as a first port of call: over half in both areas denied seeking help from any other source. Family members and other professionals were most frequently mentioned by the remainder as sources of prior help. Parents in Newpath were no more likely than those in Oldweigh to say they had sought prior help from voluntary groups or projects.

Parents often found it hard to say what their expectations of help had been. In many cases they did not seem to have very clear ideas of what could be done. The most frequently expressed expectation, among those who had formulated any, was for some sort of material help; next came information, advice or intervention on the family's behalf with another agency; about 10 per cent had most hoped for help in controlling a child, or actually removing a child; only seven per cent said they had most hoped for some sort of family counselling. There were no significant differences between the areas.

We have already seen that the majority of parents and social workers described the reason for referral in terms of financial difficulties (and that parents generally came from a particularly disadvantaged group in the population), and we have described how the pressures operating on duty workers tended to limit their assessments to clear descriptions of the presenting problem. Workers did not wish to uncover problems for which they could offer no help and many had learned in training to beware of looking beyond presenting practical problems for other kinds of family difficulties which clients did not acknowledge. However, as researchers we were interested in the extent to which parents were approaching social services *solely* on account of poverty and lack of material resources, and we therefore invited them to disclose to us problems of a more general nature which they had not necessarily mentioned at referral. The Family Problem Questionnaire was used for this purpose.

Financial and Non-Financial Problems

The separate scales did throw some light on the extent to which families were contacting social services solely because of financial problems. About 13 per cent in both areas had low scores on the Finances scale and on the non-financial scales: they apparently had few problems of any sort. Just under a third had high scores on Finances but low scores on non-financial scales: they appeared to have financial problems only. Only 12 per cent of the referrals had non-financial problems only. The largest group of referrals (some 40 per cent in both areas) reported a combination of financial and non-financial difficulties.

Although the majority of parents described the reason for referral to social services in terms of financial or material difficulties, and few said they expected help with personal or family relationship difficulties, the results on the Family Problem Questionnaire gave a rather different picture. More than half were aware of many difficulties in their social and family relationships (often combined with severe financial problems). However, they usually did not see social services as a potential source of help with non-material problems, and duty social workers did not look beyond the first presented problem.

A case example may serve to illustrate this point:

The family included Mr A (40), Mrs A (19) and their daughter aged 18 months. The couple came to the area office complaining that the neighbours were making their life impossible. Mr A had recently been struck in a violent dispute. Mrs A was pregnant again and worried about her health. The duty officer explained that social services could not assist them to get a house transfer and advised consulting the doctor and a solicitor. The duty officer did not enquire further about the family's problems.

When the research worker visited she found the family living in unsatisfactory conditions without a bed, cooker or domestic appliances. Mr A was unemployed. Mrs A said that she had been in care for many years. Her father had suggested she go to social services for help this time because of the disturbed state she was in. However she felt somewhat dissatisfied with the results of her visit to the office. The family scored high on objective indices of disadvantage and vulnerability. Mrs A had high scores on the Malaise Inventory and on four scales of the Family Problem Questionnaire. Mrs A described a relatively large network of people she could turn to for help in different areas of her life, but she also had a number of conflictful relationships, including those with her husband and father.

Four months later, at follow-up, Mrs A felt her problems were worse. She now had a new baby and there was double pressure. She had no help from social services but the NSPCC had called to investigate her care of the children. She felt the NSPCC worker was too nosey and could find nothing helpful in her contact with him. However she was getting support from the health visitor. The family's material conditions had improved and although Mrs A said that overall her problems were worse, her scores on the Malaise Inventory and the Family Problem Questionnaire were somewhat lower.

The case illustrates the extent to which area team duty officers were forced to respond only to the client's immediately presented practical problem. As in this case, there was often little social services could do to alter the material situation. Because duty workers did not generally take their assessments any further than this, opportunities for intervening early in high-risk situations might be lost.

Contact with Other Organised Support

In the first interview, and again at follow-up, parents were asked to identify from a precoded list the professional and voluntary services they had contacted in the previous month. The researchers expected that families in Newpath might have more contact with voluntary supportive resources. If Newpath families were not in contact with family projects at the time of their referral, then they might be linked to them as a result of referral. There proved to be no differences between families in the two areas in their contacts with general practitioners, health visitors, psychiatrists, the police or the probation service. There were indeed some differences in contacts with voluntary services, in the predicted direction, but the picture was a little more complicated than we had allowed for (Table 8vi).

Table 8vi
Referred Families' Contact with Supportive Resources

	Month Before Referral		4 Months After Referral	
	% In Contact			
	Oldweigh (71)	Newpath (72)	Oldweigh (61)	Newpath (61)
Day Nursery/School[1]	4	8	2	6
Child Minder[1]	4	8	2	19*
Play/M & T Group[1]	44	38	52	35
Home-Start[1]	2	4	4	7
Neigh/Family Centre	7	17	5	7
Youth Club	3	11	0	15*
Marriage Guidance	0	1	0	10*
Other	10	24*	7	20

1. Families not containing under-fives excluded from base.
* Statistically significant difference between Oldweigh and Newpath.

In Newpath, as expected, families were in touch with more voluntary agencies and groups. However, in neither area did the overall number of contacts with voluntary agencies appear to increase as a result of the referral. The mean number before referral was 0.79 in Oldweigh and 1.12 in Newpath. After four months the figures were 0.72 and 1.08. Thus referral to a social worker did not increase the average number of links between families and other sources of support in the community. Resources whose take-up did seem to increase following referral were, in Newpath only, child minding and marriage guidance; and in Oldweigh, playgroups. While we had expected that families in Newpath would be linked to a locally-based family centre as a result of referral, the trend if anything seemed to be in the other direction. Seventeen per cent said they had contacted a family project in the month before the referral, compared to seven per cent four months afterwards. This might suggest that the voluntary centres were linking people to statutory services, rather than the other way round.

Social Workers and Resources
The researchers expected that in Newpath, where great effort had gone into building up a network of local family support resources, the social workers would express more positive views towards preventive work; that they would incline more towards a community social work philosophy; and that they would be working in new ways which involved more contact with volunteers and self-help groups in the community.

In each area, before data collection began, we asked social services staff to complete a questionnaire on their knowledge and use of community resources and their attitudes to social work practice. In both areas, approximately 90 per cent of staff currently in post returned completed forms. At first sight, the results suggested that there were indeed some differences in the predicted direction. The social workers in Newpath had made significantly more use of family support resources in the previous month. As Table 8vii illustrates, part of this difference was due to their greater use of welfare rights advice and family centres provided by voluntary bodies and not available to anything like the same extent to the social workers in Oldweigh. But in Newpath, workers also made more use of social services resources, such as short-term fostering and special child-minders, to support families. The main difference between social work practice in the two areas, therefore, may have been less in the workers' use of voluntary resources, than in the way they were organised (specialised versus generic) and in their ability to exploit additional departmental resources.

Social workers in Newpath were no more likely than those in Oldweigh to report themselves as working with volunteers or self-help groups. In Newpath, eight per cent had supervised volunteers, compared with nine per cent in Oldweigh; 11 per cent in Newpath had used volunteers with children 'at risk' compared with 19 per cent in Oldweigh. Although 30 per cent had worked with self-help groups compared with only 12 per

Table 8vii
Differences between Social Workers Use of Family Support Resources in Oldweigh and Newpath

Type of Resource	Oldweigh	Newpath
	% Contacting Resource in Previous Month	
Welfare Rights Advice	10	41*
Family Centre	3	41**
NSPCC	39	11*
Child Minder	10	63**
Short-Term Fostering	23	59**
BASE: WORKERS WITH CASELOAD	32	31

  * Statistically significant at 5% level
** Statistically significant at 1% level

cent, the difference was not statistically significant. Expressed attitudes to the involvement of volunteers were generally positive. Three-quarters in Newpath, and two-thirds in Oldweigh, thought that volunteers could be involved in casework; similar proportions thought that volunteers were reliable. However, over half in both areas thought that volunteers should not be used in situations that might be risky; and that the use of volunteers caused extra work for the social worker. If volunteers are perceived as somewhat burdensome, then hard-pressed social workers may well avoid using them.

The workers in the two areas also expressed similar attitudes to preventive social work (Table 8viii).

Table 8viii
Social Workers' Attitudes to Preventive Work in Oldweigh and Newpath

	Oldweigh (35)	Newpath (31)
	% Agreeing	
Shortage of resources makes it very difficult to undertake non-statutory work.	86	74
Preventive social work is a luxury not a priority for social services staff.	57	38
There needs to be big changes in our organisation so that our team can spend more time in preventive work.	91	83
I would like to do preventive work but I don't have time.	77	67

Staff in both areas tended to feel that they were hindered from undertaking preventive work with families by shortage of time and resources. Several staff added comments which illustrate the likely effects on morale of this situation.

> To see people who desperately need help and know there are absolutely no resources available is very frustratiing and adds stress to an already stressful job. We can then only help when situations reach crisis point. (*Oldweigh*)

> There is little personal satisfaction in only providing a partial service or in knowing the client sometimes waits too long *ie* has to reach crisis before any service is provided. (*Oldweigh*)

> There's no time at all for liaison work with other agencies, which is vital if you are to know your patch and work effectively for clients. At present I feel I spend most of my time trying to fend off work instead of doing the job properly. (*Newpath*)

The resources most often mentioned as lacking or in very short supply in Oldweigh were day nursery provision and a social services Family Resource Centre with facilities for whole families. In Newpath, nursery provision was also most often felt to be lacking. Although there was already a network of locally-based, voluntary family projects, many social workers still often felt the lack of a social services family centre, which could be used for assessment and family treatment. As one such worker put it:

> Professional social workers [are needed] to cope with professional demands of work that voluntary agencies cannot be involved in—including more fieldworkers and in particular a professionally run family centre working in planned ways with families at risk.

Thus, although social workers in both areas generally took a positive view of preventive work, they tended to feel that they themselves were rarely in a position to undertake it. One way out of this dilemma might have been to limit their involvement with individual clients in order to free time to develop additional resources in the community itself. The researchers expected that social workers in Newpath would feel more sympathy for this approach. Table 8ix shows the questions with which we attempted to test whether they were in fact more 'community-minded'.

The social workers in the two areas appeared to have rather similar attitudes. Most agreed that they *should* be undertaking community development tasks, but they did not want this to be at the expense of the interests of individual families with problems—their clients. They tended not to agree with the view that investment of resources in 'casualties' should have a lower priority. For workers carrying caseloads, it was certainly true that setting aside time for community development activities would have meant giving less time to individual families with pressing problems, so that there was a real conflict to be faced.

Table 8ix
'Community-Mindedness' in Oldweigh and Newpath

	Oldweigh (35)	Newpath (31)
	% Agreeing	
There are untapped resources in the community that social workers should be using.	71	93
Social workers can achieve more by working with self-help groups than by working with identified individuals or families with problems.	29	32
Social workers must give less time to the rescue of casualties and more to supporting the community's efforts to help itself.	31	39
Social workers should put more effort into developing community resources.	74	76
If social workers get involved in community development individual cases will lose out.	46	27
Developing partnerships with outside agencies is so time-consuming that it is impossible to do it within ordinary social work practice.	37	42

In summary, there appeared to be few differences between the attitudes or reported practice of the social workers in the two areas in relation to 'community-mindedness' or preventive social work. Although the social workers in Newpath did not appear to have deliberately changed their practice in order to exploit the wealth of family projects that had been built up in the community, they were more often in contact with these resources than was the case in Oldweigh. However, they may not have seen the existence of these new resources as particularly relevant to their own tasks with families, and many continued to see a need for a different type of family centre—run by professionals and used by them to assist in their central task of protecting children deemed to be at risk.

Help from Social Services Department

What help from the social services department did families in the two areas receive as a result of referral? Table 8x summarises the services that were given to families in the two areas over the four month period, under these headings. The differences in the ways the teams were organised in the two areas show clearly. In Oldweigh there was a definite policy of clearing up as many referrals as possible within the duty system on the same day. In Newpath, on the other hand, there were short-term assessment workers in each sub-team who specialised in following up referrals to make fuller assessments than were possible in one day. Thus, in Newpath families were much more likely to be allocated to caseloads, and were also somewhat more likely to receive additional supportive services. However, in neither area did allocation to a caseload often lead to an extended period of contact with a social worker.

At follow-up, 31 per cent in Oldweigh and 43 per cent in Newpath described some contact with a social worker in the four months after referral. It was usually quite limited: in Oldweigh over two-thirds, and in Newpath a half, had seen the social worker once or twice only. Allocation often served an administrative purpose—checking on eligibility, for example—and involved no more than one-off contact.

In Oldweigh, by far the commonest supportive service offered was help with playgroup fees (received by 25 per cent). By contrast, in Newpath small sums of money were given directly to 18 per cent (compared to only one per cent in Oldweigh), while financial help tied to playgroup fees went to 13 per cent. There was legal intervention in under five per cent in both areas. Residential care was very rare, but in Newpath 16 per cent received short-term fostering or special minding, compared to some three per cent in Oldweigh. Family Aides were a scarce resource in both areas and were received by only one or two of the sample.

Table 8x
Contact with Social Services in Four Months After Referral

	Oldweigh (72) %	Newpath (72) %
No Further Contact	38	34
Referral/Duty Only	17	0
Allocated Only	14	22
Allocated plus Other Service	11	38*
Other Service Only	20	6*

* Statistically significantly difference

While there were marked differences in service delivery patterns in the two areas, they probably had little to do with the existence or otherwise of community-based supportive resources. They were more likely to be caused by the different structures and the different levels of resources within the departments themselves. In Newpath there was a specialised team, and there were also more social services resources for families. The social workers here appeared to use their resources rather differently, making more use of direct payments for example, and less use of help with playgroup fees. In Newpath, both families and social workers were in touch with more voluntary groups than was the case in Oldweigh, but the social workers did not appear to be linking families to community resources they had previously been unaware of.

CHAPTER 9

Referred Families:
Outcomes After Four Months

This chapter will describe changes in family problems four months after referral to social services, and whether, as predicted, outcomes were different in Newpath, the area with the most developed family support provision.

Outcomes after four months were measured by repeating the Malaise Inventory and the Family Problem Questionnaire. In addition parents were asked for their opinions about any changes and were questioned about their satisfaction with the help they had received from social services.

Oldweigh and Newpath: Differences in Outcome
In Newpath, parents showed significant improvement on measures of social contact, parenting, finances and malaise. In Oldweigh, the improvement in these areas only reached significance in the case of parenting. By the time of the follow-up, there were statistically significant differences between the scores of parents in Oldweigh and Newpath on the Malaise Inventory and the social contact measure, after controlling for the levels of problem at referral.

In Oldweigh, 21 per cent of families had a 'good' outcome after four months, 33 per cent had a 'fair' outcome, and 46 per cent had a 'poor' outcome. In Newpath, the corresponding proportions were 29 per cent, 43 per cent and 28 per cent. Thus, while 46 per cent had a poor overall outcome in Oldweigh, only 28 per cent did so in Newpath—a difference that was verging on statistical significance ($p = .06$)

Parents' own opinions were in agreement with these findings in that more of those in Newpath said that the family difficulties were 'better' at the time of follow-up (61 per cent versus 42 per cent $p < .05$). More parents in Newpath also reported themselves as 'satisfied' or 'very satisfied' with the help they had received from social services (53 per cent versus 42 per cent) and fewer as dissatisfied (25 per cent versus 39 per cent).

The follow-up interview had been planned to examine with parents the aspects of social work help that they had found particularly helpful—what aspects of the relationship with the social worker had

Table 9i
Problem Scores and Malaise: Referral and Four Months Later

	Oldweigh (61)		Newpath (61)[2]	
	Time 1	Time 2	Time 1	Time 2
	Mean Scores			
Social Contact	16.8	15.7	15.7	13.5***
Parenting	21.1	18.6*	19.6	17.6**
Finances	17.1	15.7	18.0	15.4***
Health	6.6	6.6	7.3	7.3
Marital[1]	9.5	8.0	9.1	9.2
Malaise	8.6	8.1	7.7	6.0**

[1]Married/Cohabiting only
[2]Some data missing on 2 cases
 Paired t-test: * P.05; ** P < .01; *** P < .001

A summary indicator of overall outcomes was devised as follows:

* Good: Low scores on all family problem scales and a malaise score of less than 7.

* Fair: *Either* low scores on all family problem scales *or* a malaise score of less than 7.

* Poor: High scores on one or more family problems scales *and* a malaise Inventory score
           of 7 or more.

actually proved to be supportive, from the parents' viewpoint. Since allocation to a social worker often involved no more than a short period of investigation for a definite administrative purpose, the sample did not prove a good one in which to examine social work practice in any depth. Table 9ii sets out the views of the minority of parents who reported any extended contact with a social worker. They were asked, 'During your contact with the social worker do you think you are/were being helped by:'. There followed a list of 18 specific 'helping' activities, for example, 'Knowing you can rely on the social worker to visit regularly'. The information was asked to rate each one as:

* 0 Does/Did Not Happen

* 1 Yes Definitely Helped

* 2 Yes Possibly Helped

* 3 No Possibly Not Helpful

* 4 No Definitely Not Helpful

The activities were intended to be representative of three broad areas of help: friendship; linking clients to other sources of support; attempting to bring about change in behaviour. In both areas, 'change-oriented' activities were most often reported, though they were not necessarily experienced as helpful. Contrary to expectation, Newpath clients were no more likely to report activities of the 'linking' type.

In summary, there was consistent evidence from the various measures of outcome that the referred families in Newpath appeared to be dealing with their problems rather more successfully than those in Oldweigh. In particular, four months after referral, Newpath parents had significantly lower malaise scores and significantly fewer social contact problems than Oldweigh parents.

Table 9ii
Parents' Views of Family Support Activities by Social Workers

Activity	Oldweigh (19)			Newpath (26)		
	Did Not Happen %	Helpful %	Un-helpful %	Did Not Happen %	Helpful %	Un-helpful %
'Friendship'						
Regular visits	63	21	16	46	46	8
Chat/TV	63	26	0	73	27	0
Take chi. out	84	0	16	88	12	0
Lend money, etc.	79	5	16	77	23	0
Help in house	84	0	16	96	4	0
'Linking'						
Contact Soc. Sec.	68	10	22	58	35	7
Meeting parents	68	5	27	96	4	0
Chi. meeting chi.	68	5	27	69	27	4
Outings	79	5	16	96	4	0
Other sources help	74	0	26	73	27	0
Drop-in, group att.	84	0	16	92	8	0
Joining clubs, etc.	84	5	11	92	0	8
Making new friends	79	0	21	85	15	0
'Changing'						
Talk re problems	32	32	36	35	65	0
New things chi.	58	10	32	85	11	4
Understand chi.	53	16	31	58	35	7
Understand self	47	21	32	58	27	15
Better with partner	74	5	21	73	15	12

Reasons for Differences

What were the reasons for the apparently better results in Newpath? A possible explanation might lie in the greater family support provision in Newpath, and the ability of social workers to exploit this for parents' benefit. As we have seen, however, the referred families were not linked to the new family support projects in Newpath as a result of referral to social services. Social workers were not really acting as link people in the way the researchers had expected.

It has already been demonstrated that the social services department in Newpath itself provided help to a higher proportion of referred families. Could greater improvement in Newpath have been related to direct help from social services, rather than to links with family support provision outside the department?

Who Received Help from Social Services?

The families were grouped into three clusters, described in the last chapter, according to their measured needs at the time of referral. In Oldweigh, families in the High Need group were significantly more likely to receive some service from the social services department: 53 per cent of them did so, compared to 33 per cent of those with Material Need, and only 21 per cent of the Coping group. In Newpath, there was less apparent matching of service to levels of need: 47 per cent of the High Need group received a service; 54 per cent of the Material Need group; and 42 per cent of the Coping group. Thus, the better results in Newpath were not explained by better matching of services to needs.

Improvement of Malaise

In Oldweigh, where there was no overall improvement in malaise, parents who did show improvement were no more or less likely to have received help from social services. In Newpath, we were surprised to find an association, but in the wrong direction: parents who received a service were *less* likely to show improvement in malaise. This was particularly striking for those in the 'High Need Group'. In Newpath, eight of these had received some service and nine had not. All these nine showed improvement in malaise, but only three of the eight who had received a service (Fisher's Exact Test: sig. .009). It therefore could not be argued that the greater degree of improvement in malaise scores in Newpath was due to social services' intervention.

There was also no tendency for parents who had been in contact with a larger number of community groups to show greater improvement in malaise. Therefore the greater number of such contacts in Newpath could not be the explanation for lower malaise there.

Support received from informal sources—family, friends and neigh-bours—appeared more important in explaining improvement in malaise scores. Families in the High Need or Material Needs Groups tended not to improve unless at the time of referral they had named four or more people (excluding professionals) to whom they could turn for support (Table 9iii).

Table 9iii
Improvement in Malaise and Number of Informal Supporters

Number of Supporters	Mean Improvement	
	Oldweigh	Newpath
0–3	−.27(11)	.5 (6)
4–6	1.1(15)	1.4(18)
7+	1.2(10)	4.1(17)

Base numbers (High Need and Material Need Groups) in brackets

In Newpath, where the effect of informal support was particularly marked, there were fewer parents in the High Need Groups who named less than four informal supporters and more who had seven or more. The presence of adequate informal support at referral may have been a contributing factor in their greater improvement in emotional distress over the next four months.

In chapter 7 the strong relationship between malaise and characteristics of individual support systems was described. Parents who had few instru-mental supporters, or many conflicted relationships, or who were dissat-isfied with their support, also tended to have high malaise scores. However, the presence of these factors at referral did not predict the amount of improvement in malaise over the next four months.

Improvement in Family Problems
Families in both areas reported a significant degree of improvement in parent-child problems at the time of follow-up. In Oldweigh, families who had received practical help from the social services department were more likely to show improvement. In the 'High Need' group in Oldweigh, all eight of those who received a service showed improvement in parenting problems, compared to only three of the seven who received no service (Fisher's Exact Test: sig. .025). In Newpath, on the other hand, improvement was equally likely to occur whether or not a service had been provided. Thus, while in Oldweigh improvement in parenting problems could have been directly associated with social services practical help, this could not have been so in Newpath.

A possible explanation for this apparent contradiction might lie in the different type of services provided in the two areas. In Oldweigh, by far the most common practical service was the provision of help with play group fees. This type of help was less often given in Newpath, where more use was made of small sums of money made available under the provisions of Section 1 of the 1980 Child Care Act. It is possible that the provision of a regular (though small) grant which enables a child to attend a play group for at least one session a week has a beneficial impact on the child's behaviour and on the parent-child relationship. A small, one-off sum of money, on the other hand might not make an impact on parent-child difficulties which would still be measurable after four months.

Parents who received practical help from social services, did show significantly more improvement in financial problems. Newpath families got more financial help and showed rather more improvement.

Social services help was not related to improvement in the remaining family problem areas.

For both areas, there was a significant positive association between improvement in parenting problems (not in malaise or other family problems) and the number of reported contacts with voluntary agencies and groups in the community (P < .02). Since contact with voluntary groups was significantly more frequent in Newpath, there may have been some general effect which contributed to better outcomes there. The most important effect, however, came from the use of any day care provision—playgroups, mother and toddler groups, nurseries or nursery schools, child minders or other provision.

Parents of under-fives in both areas showed more improvement in parenting problems if they made use of any form of day-care (Table 9iv). This is consistent with the earlier finding that practical help in Oldweigh (which was generally tied to fees for playgroup attendance) appeared to have more effect on parent-child outcome than did practical help in Newpath.

Table 9iv
Improvement in Parenting Problems and Any Day-Care at Follow-Up

Improvement in Parenting	No Day Care	Any Day Care
Same/Worse	17	11
Improved	22	38
Total (Under 5s)	39	49

Chi Sq = 4.47 sig. .034
Missing data on 3 cases

In summary, although Newpath parents tended to have better outcomes four months after referral to social services, the reasons for this could not be fully established. The evidence suggested that the support of family, friends and neighbours, and the use of day care provision, might have been as or more important that the help received from social services or from organised community groups.

Factors Associated with Outcome

We have already defined a 'Good Outcome', for the purposes of this study, as consisting of few or no family problems and a parental malaise score of under seven at the time of follow-up. The main influence on outcome in this sense was the level of Need and Vulnerability present at referral: not one of the fifteen families in the High Need/High Vulnerability Group at referral had a 'good' (problem free) outcome four months later, while approaching half the 35 families in the Coping/Low Vulnerability Group at referral had a good outcome.

This very strong relationship between outcome and factors present at referral was not weakened by any of the intervening factors we tested. Thus we had to conclude that, when levels of Need and Vulnerability were controlled for, neither provision of a social service, nor number of contacts with voluntary groups, nor number of informal supporters had an effect on absolute outcome.

Table 9v illustrates the relationship between Need Group at the time of referral, overall outcome after four months and provision of social services. Although there are small differences between the outcomes of families who did and did not receive some service, they are not statistically significant, given the small numbers. However, there were some individual exceptions.

Table 9v
Outcomes After Four Months, Referral Characteristics and Service Provision

Needs	Vulnerability	Social Service		No Service	
		Outcome			
		Good/Fair %	Poor %	Good/Fair %	Poor %
High	High	30	70(10)	0	100 (5)
High	Low	33	67 (6)	27	73(11)
Material	High	73	27(11)	38	62 (8)
Material	Low	100	0 (8)	76	24(17)
Coping	High	100	0 (2)	60	40 (5)
Coping	Low	100	0(10)	80	20(25)

Base numbers in brackets

'Good' Exceptions

Case 35. In the case a playgroup leader referred Jack Roberts, aged three, after noticing bruising on his face. Jack said father had done this but had told him to say he fell out of bed. The family fell into the High Need/High Vulnerability Group at referral. Mrs Roberts had been known to social services in another area in a previous marriage, when her children had been taken into care. The health visitor had made an earlier referral expressing concern over Jack's treatment by his father. Mrs Roberts had high scores on the family problem scales. She had major financial difficulties. Her relationship with husband was tense and she was afraid of his violence. However, she had good informal support from a large network.

At follow-up, this High Need family did not have, as might have been expected, a poor outcome: there was a marked improvement in family problems. The social services had taken legal proceedings to protect Jack, who had been taken into care and fostered for a time. Mr Roberts had been prosecuted and placed on probation. Although Mrs Roberts was not happy with social services intervention and the temporary separation from Jack with inadequate visiting arrangements, she acknowledged that its effects had been good, since husband was now better with Jack and with the family generally.

Case 321. Mrs Bateson and her cohabitee came to social services when she was discharged from hospital after having taken an overdose. They had previously sought help from the department for serious fuel debts and Social Security difficulties. There were two children under five, one of whom was difficult to manage. Mrs B. had taken the overdose as a way of drawing attention to her difficulties and her need for a housing transfer.

At follow-up Mrs Bateson's problems were much improved. She reported having regular weekly contact with the social worker, by phone or visit, which had helped quite a lot. Social services had given financial help with playgroup fees and also organised speech therapy for the older child and helped with getting the family on the phone, which had reduced Mrs Bateson's feelings of isolation. The social worker had also helped the couple to get along better: 'She does listen to both sides—not just siding with me'. Her only complaint was that the social worker was not instantly available when she needed her: 'If she can't come out [immediately] by the time she does come I have got myself in a state'.

These cases were very unusual in that the social workers concerned had been able to make comprehensive assessments of family problems and then provide appropriate packages of services. If the level of service found in these two 'exceptions' had been more generally available, would there have been more families in High Need Groups who managed a good outcome?

CHAPTER 10

Conclusions

In Part 1 of this book, ideas about the purposes of preventive social work with families and children were reviewed. A distinction was drawn between provision intended to achieve specific preventive ends, (such as preventing the need for permanent separation of children from their own families), and more broadly-based family support provision. Specific preventive provision was seen as selective, targeted at families with already identified special needs. In contrast, locally-based family support services intended to compensate for material disadvantage and help children in need to achieve their full potential, were seen as open to all families, though best sited in localities containing many needy ones.

Family Support and Specific Prevention
Under the Children Act (1989) local authorities have responsibilities to make provision available under both these headings. Under Part III of the Act, local authorities have a general duty to safeguard and promote the welfare of children in their area who are in need; and, so far as consistent with that aim, to promote their upbringing in their own families. Local authorities can provide, or arrange for others to provide, services to families, not just to children; and in Schedule 2 of the Act a wide range of family support services is specified. But local authorities also retain specific duties to prevent the need for children to be brought before courts; and to prevent children suffering neglect or ill-treatment.

One way for local authorities to carry out their duty to promote the welfare of children in need through the provision of family support is through a strategy of building up locally-based resources in areas with many needs. It was argued in Part 1 that local authorities should engage in this type of neighbourhood-based family support mainly indirectly, through their support for independently-run voluntary and informal groups. At this level, local authorities should not be specifying in any detail the kinds of activity or forms of organisation that might develop in response to local needs.

Authorities should, however, retain more direct responsibility for specific prevention. They could provide special services themselves to children and families where serious problems had already been identified.

They could buy in services from other organisations, using contracts and detailed specifications, and monitoring the extent to which the specified objectives were met.

Within this kind of overall strategy a number of differently organised, or relatively unorganised, groups would be involved in the provision of family support within a social services area. A large proportion of the funding, however, would have to continue to come from statutory services.

Within this strategy there would also be some development in the role of social workers themselves. They would need to be skilled at linking children and families with services outside the direct control of the social services department. Greater emphasis would need to be placed on skills to do with assessment and monitoring of needs and bringing together different kinds of service provision in appropriate individual packages.

There would be more need to evaluate the effectiveness and cost of different kinds of provision. Services intended to achieve specific preventive ends should be judged according to their success in achieving those ends. For example, the success of a service intended to improve parenting skills and reduce violent treatment of children must be assessed against evidence of change in those specific areas. Locally-based family support provision should be judged against different criteria: for example, the extent to which it contributes to the resources of a neighbourhood; whether it can link people with each other and provide a reservoir of supplies for families to draw on when they are hit by external stress; whether it can divert people away from inappropriate dependence on statutory agencies.

Aims of the Study

The book told a story about the implementation in one social services area—Newpath—of a family support policy that emphasised the development of independent, locally-based resources. Newpath was exceptional in having developed a series of family projects on estates considered to have special needs. In contrast to Oldweigh, a demographically similar social services area in another authority, it provided a case study of partnership between statutory and large voluntary organisations and local communities. It was hoped to draw from Newpath's experiences some more general lessons about means of developing and managing new resources for family support; about links between voluntary projects and statutory agencies; and about changing roles of social workers in response to new patterns of provision.

As well as the descriptive study of family support resources, there was a complementary study of families, based on a three-way comparison: between families with children referred to social services in Newpath, and the comparison area, Oldweigh; and randomly selected families with children in the population of Newpath.

The Family Projects

The resource study was principally concerned with seven family projects that had been developed in Newpath between 1981 and 1988. Two were more specialised projects, aimed at specific kinds of family who were referred by other agencies for services. Five were neighbourhood family projects (one of which did not become fully operational until the research had ended), placed on estates considered to have many needs. Although most of these latter accepted referrals, they were open to anyone in their local areas. The first two projects, therefore, could be seen as examples of the specific type of preventive provision discussed above; while the other five (the neighbourhood family projects) were examples of broad-based family support provision.

The development of the various projects was described in chapter 4. Four national children's charities had been involved, as well as Newpath council, the county council, and professionals working in the statutory services — health, education and social services. It was no coincidence that all this provision had come about in Newpath. Its local authority proved to be most unusual in the level of its commitment to community development, maintained over decades. The county council also, though not a high-spending authority, placed a high value on developing partnership with the voluntary sector.

When the neighbourhood family projects were first planned in the 1970s and early 1980s, they were expected to make a contribution to the provision of day care—for working parents as well as for so-called priority groups. As the neighbourhood projects developed, however, they no longer wanted or were expected to provide day care services. A stronger emphasis was placed on loosely-defined aims to do with community development—fostering of self-help groups, advice and advocacy provision.

Chapter 5 described the projects, as they were in 1988. The staff in the neighbourhood family projects were strongly committed to the value of an open-door approach, which blurred distinctions between 'helpers' and 'helped', stressed personal growth, and opened up opportunities for users to participate in the running of the project. The two more specialised projects saw themselves as different from, but complementary to, the neighbourhood centres. They considered that they were focussing on particular needs, or on people particularly lacking in skills and confidence who would simply not have gone to a neighbourhood project, but who might do so in the future.

The vast majority of users of the projects comprised white women and their children. Men were seldom attracted. Although Newpath itself had only a small proportion of minority group residents, an even smaller proportion appeared to be using any of the family projects.

Staff in the projects had a variety of qualifications and previous experiences. Only one project had a clear policy of appointing local staff: here, staff had come from users of the project itself.

All but one project made considerable use of volunteers, who undertook such tasks as running welfare rights advice points, play schemes, shops, outings, discussion groups; and individual befriending. Most projects had to work hard to attract volunteers but their success, both in recruiting and in retaining them, was striking. All projects provided training and support for volunteers. The main distinction was between projects where the role of volunteer was clearly set off from that of project user; and those where such a clear separation of roles was seen as undesirable.

The neighbourhood family projects, in keeping with their open-door policies and broad aims, were providing a much wider range of activities than the two more specialised projects. However, befriending and counselling services for individual families under stress (often referred by statutory agencies) were occupying a good part of staff time in all the projects. The neighbourhood projects also provided social activities, advice points, opportunities for the exchange of resources and broadly-defined educational activities.

There was no uniform pattern of project management. Local management had clear advantages in terms of local accountability and opportunities for users to participate, but there were also a good many problems. The composition of a committee drawn from local volunteers inevitably changed fairly often. Committee members often had no specific management skills and the time they could give to training (and indeed the resources to pay for it) were limited. Staff found it difficult both to support a committee in its management functions, and to be employed by it. There was some agreement that local management would become more viable if there was a means whereby projects could have continuing access to specific management support services, such as personnel and accountancy.

Similarities and Differences

There was more common ground than difference between all seven family projects, and especially between the five neighbourhood ones. However, there did seem to be an underlying cause of variation: the extent to which projects saw themselves as providing direct services to families in need. The balance between a 'service-giving' philosophy, and one that was more concerned with community development, seemed to influence a number of other factors. The role differentiation between staff, volunteers and users; the balance between different kinds of activities; the management structure and the opportunities for users and local people to participate in management, all seemed related to this underlying dimension.

The right balance between the needs of individual families in distress, and the needs of local families in general seemed difficult to achieve. It might be thought that the balance should be differently struck in the two specialised projects as opposed to the neighbourhood projects. While this was true to some extent, it seemed that none of the neighbourhood projects was yet becoming much involved in broader issues that affected families in general—such as provision for the under-fives, for example, or the way families were represented at case conferences, to take another kind of example. Project leaders were aware of issues that were of general relevance to parents, such as, for example, the need for better communica-tion with schools. However, they were more likely to become involved at an individual level—by representing or advocating for a particular family.

Relationship with Statutory Agencies

This 'individual' bias was clearly seen in the relationships between projects and statutory services. As yet, even in the neighbourhood projects, they seemed to be mainly concerned with the process of making and receiving referrals of individual families. There was little or no joint assessment of the needs of families in the local neighbourhoods, with the projects playing a more general advocacy role.

Representatives from statutory agencies were serving on the manage-ment or advisory committees of all the projects, but some local managers felt that the level of representation was not entirely appropriate. Represen-tatives tended to be drawn from the fieldwork services—'carers', who were well-suited to providing casework backup but less equipped with specific management skills. Only one neighbourhood family project had a nominated 'link' social worker. This was the only project with a definite view that links with statutory agencies should be a means to improving mutual understanding and making better-informed policies; rather than a means whereby agencies obtained support for individual families.

Another example of successful 'structural' liaison was the provision in another neighbourhood project of a regular Housing Advice Point, run by a worker from the housing department and project volunteers. This appeared to have led to changes on the estate, such as the provision of rubbish skips, which benefited families in general as well as the individual who sought advice.

Funders

Funds for the setting-up of the family projects came from many different sources: central government (under the Urban Aid and Opportunities for Volunteering programmes); local government; the health authority; national children's charities; and corporate charity. But national funding that had been available to new ventures was not available in perpetuity. All the projects succeeded in establishing themselves, but they were then faced with the struggle to find new sources of funding in order to keep going. National voluntary bodies were as unwilling as national government to tie up funds in established work.

'Partnership' between statutory and voluntary sectors in funding appeared to be difficult to maintain beyond a strictly limited time-scale. National voluntary agencies had their own priorities and might unilaterally change their policies. There appeared to have been such a change in relation to family centres, which were no longer seen as exciting new developments. Thus, if the family projects were to continue beyond a development stage, local authorities would have to assume the major responsibilities for funding them. In the original funding 'partnership', mutual expectations between the statutory and voluntary sectors were perhaps not sufficiently clarified and agreements binding on both sides were not reached. As the main responsibility passed to local government, local statutory agencies and local corporate sources, there were encouraging signs that the somewhat vague notions of 'partnership' were being replaced by a more business-like approach which might actually give the projects more security and stability.

The danger that clearer contractual expectations and obligations might threaten the autonomy of the voluntary sector, forcing upon it a bureaucratic structure, and reducing its flexibility and capacity for innovation, was acknowledged by statutory funders. Most projects felt that at present funders had little influence on their actual operation, but they all admitted that funders could in effect 'pull the plug' if they became displeased. The existence of a strong intermediary organisation in the Newpath Voluntary Services Centre was important in promoting dialogue between projects and funders, as well as in providing support services for the projects themselves.

Any continuing involvement of national voluntary organisations in neighbourhood family projects appeared likely to hold back moves towards the development of local management. Although local management had its difficulties, most family projects and statutory agencies agreed that it was the right way forwards and that means should be found to strengthen the local committees. Since the national voluntaries were accountable for the way their funds were spent, it was difficult for them to relinquish control to a local management group. This limited local accountability and the projects' ability to respond to changing local needs. For example, a neighbourhood which at one stage had many young families and corresponding needs for support for under-fives, might have a different age-structure not so many years later, with correspondingly different priorities. Yet a children's charity could not countenance its funding being switched to, say, support for families caring for elderly or disabled members.

Thus there were a number of reasons for believing that 'partnership' between national voluntaries and local statutory services might not provide an appropriate framework for the continuing operation of independent neighbourhood family projects. However, for projects that provide a defined service to a particular group of families, 'partnership' seemed to work well.

Accountability and Evaluation

Independent family projects that depend heavily on state funds may be seen as a contradiction in terms. However, given goodwill on the part of the funders, clearer contracts between the two sides could actually strengthen the autonomy of the voluntary sector. For example, the neighbourhood family projects appeared to be holding back from advocacy on behalf of community needs in favour of individualised support for families referred by other agencies. They believed that by so doing they were meeting funders' expectations, yet there was evidence that some funders took a broader view of the functions of neighbourhood projects. Through a contractual process, mutual expectations could be negotiated and clarified. Provided a central 'core' was maintained, it might also be appropriate for statutory funders to contract for certain specific services, while recognising that projects would undertake other activities with other funding. Statutory funding need not lead inevitably to domination by the state.

Nevertheless, projects would have to recognise the need to account for their activities, and thus to build into their operations procedures for monitoring and evaluation. In return, funders would need to recognise this as a legitimate cost, that should not have to come out of core funding intended to maintain project activities.

Why should statutory agencies be ready to transfer part of their funds, especially in times of scarcity, to small, independent, family projects? The advantages of voluntary sector provision have been comprehensively reviewed by Knapp *et al.* (1988). The family projects offered many of the benefits identified in their review. They provided more choice; they offered local citizens opportunities to contribute and participate; they could be more flexible than statutory services, and respond in innovative ways to locally expressed needs. They had the potential to become forceful advocates on behalf of local needs, and so improve the performance of the statutory services themselves. These benefits, however, depended on the projects' success in establishing themselves in their local areas.

The Projects and the Local Community

Chapter 8 described the findings of a sample survey of families in the local population, which was intended to investigate this point. The aim was to find out how widely the new projects were known, and which families were using them. The results suggested that approaching one in two families with children under 14 had heard of a family project, but only a small minority of these actually made contact. An important reason for *not* doing so was the judgment that projects were for families with problems: they were not relevant unless a family was in difficulties.

Projects were attracting families under stress: only four per cent of couples with few social needs had ever contacted one, but twenty-nine per cent of lone parents had done so. The projects, therefore, were successful in attracting a higher proportion of families with most needs, (though not exclusively them), but this very success probably limited their appeal among local families in general.

The success of the family projects in attracting disadvantaged families was the more striking in comparison to the relative failure of other forms of provision to do so. Playgroups, for example, a more frequently used form of provision which had the most satisfied users, differentially attracted 'advantaged' families.

There was evidence therefore that the family projects were gradually establishing themselves and becoming well-known in their own areas. They had strengthened local community resources, by providing new activities and advice points, by drawing in new volunteers, and by opening up new opportunities for local people. It was clear that families with many needs were not deterred from making use of open-access neighbourhood projects. Family projects benefited a mix of different types of user. There was some evidence, though, of a certain degree of stigma attaching to the projects: they were seen by some as relevant only to 'problem' families.

Professional Social Work Role

Small teams of paid staff were needed in the new family projects, but they were rarely led by professional social workers. Family projects generally did not want social workers to support and guide them in their own activities, but, on occasions they did express needs for professional backup. No family project, for example, saw itself as competent to assume responsibility for child protection.

Staff within statutory agencies could benefit from working with family projects. Managers could use their input to plan and deliver better services. Field social workers could become less isolated and agency-bound, and learn to understand people's needs and support systems better. In return, social workers could provide a necessary professional back-up, offering consultation, helping with training, arranging specialised services, and using their skills (and legal powers) directly on rare occasions, when requested.

Families Referred to Social Services

When samples of families referred to social services were compared with randomly selected families, the differences in family composition and material needs were striking. Half the referred families were headed by lone parents (usually divorced women in their late twenties and early thirties). Many more referred families (couples as well as lone parents) were disadvantaged in housing, and in access to employment and consumer goods.

A high proportion of randomly selected parents interviewed in the community survey saw the social services department as essentially a financial relief agency: there was still considerable confusion between its functions and those of social security. In the referred samples, material problems were the commonest reason for contact with social services, and financial help or advice the most often expressed expectation.

Social workers have often been accused of overlooking material problems in the quest for underlying emotional difficulties, but this was not true of the workers in this study. They usually took clients' presentations at face value, without enquiring into difficulties that were not spontaneously mentioned.

Family social work in these area teams almost always meant work with a restricted range of poor families. Many clients in financial difficulties were turning to social services, either as a first port of call, or after being turned away by social security. This fact confronted staff with all the difficulties of 'poor relief' discussed in Part 1 of the book. How far should professional staff in social services become involved with poor families in financial difficulties but without other serious family problems? Some argue that advocacy and material help should have a high priority among social workers' functions. Others maintain that responsibility for income maintenance must be laid firmly on social security; and that social services departments have neither the resources nor the powers to make more than a token contribution to the plight of poor families in general. Observation of advice and advocacy provided in the new family projects suggested that trained volunteers, backed up by a good law centre, were able to offer a better quality of service than could ever have been possible as part of routine office duty in a busy social services department. Thus workers in social services might achieve more for poor clients by linking them with appropriate external resources than by attempting to provide welfare rights advice themselves.

Non-Financial Family Problems

Parents in referred families also differed sharply from the comparison community parents in the extent to which they were burdened with a whole range of problems in addition to financial ones. In referred families, the main parent was much more likely to be suffering from depressed mood and to describe a range of severe family problems to do with relationships and health as well as money. Although their personal support systems were no smaller, they felt more isolated and worse supported. They were more often in conflict with others, especially close family members. Yet these referred parents rarely saw the social services department as a potential source of help with non-material problems. Duty social workers usually did not carry out the kinds of assessment which would have revealed other difficulties. The exception was for the minority of referrals where child abuse was mentioned, when thorough investigation was usual. Non-financial family problems, which did not involve child abuse or neglect, were least likely to lead to the offer of any service after the referral.

The conditions of duty work, described in chapter 3, made it very difficult to carry out more than a superficial assessment in the majority of cases. To do more than this, the departments would have to move to a more controlled and selective form of practice, so that social workers had more protection from the pressures of uncontrolled demand. The social workers in the study were expected to do all manner of tasks that others might have performed equally well or better—an observation that has been repeatedly made (see for example, Goldberg & Warburton, 1979).

If clients needing only expert financial advice and advocacy had been diverted to a more appropriate source, professional social workers might have been able to devote more time and energy to families with serious parent-child difficulties. In this study, although the families with the greatest measured needs got more help, it usually consisted of a brief contact, often for an administrative purpose. Giving more priority to families with a range of severe problems would necessitate cutting back on the provision of general advice services by trained social workers.

Social Workers and Family Support Resources

In contrast to the argument of the previous paragraphs, the Barclay Committee (1982), in its views on community social work, appeared to suggest that social workers might withdraw from 'the rescue of casualties' in favour of identifying and strengthening natural sources of help within communities. As discussed in chapter 8, the majority of social workers in the two research areas was not willing to make such a choice. Furthermore, in Newpath inexorable pressures from rising numbers of child abuse referrals prevented the implementation of even a modest switch of social work time towards community activities. The social workers in the two research areas were probably not unusual in their views that, while strengthening the community's own resources was desirable, they themselves could not take much part in these activities without sacrificing their specialised work with individual families in serious difficulties. They were usually knowledgeable about local preventive resources and groups, which they saw as potentially useful to them in their work with families. They were willing to act as referral agents but most did not seem to consider it feasible to combine their primary casework responsibilities with a more active role in developing or linking with voluntary provision.

In Newpath, the social services area manager had played a key role in the creation of a network of local family projects, as was described in chapter 4. But the other side of these community-oriented policies—the change in roles of social services staff—had never been implemented.

The differences the researchers had expected to see in social work practice in an area where many neighbourhood-based family projects had been successfully developed, did not materialise. Opportunities for linking parents to resources they were not already using (especially in the case of under-fives provision) appeared to be missed.

There were probably several reasons for this. One was undoubtedly the siege mentality which grew under the pressure of child abuse referrals. Then too, the fact that structural changes in the organisation of the area team were not made, that it remained centralised, and that no induction into new models of work was attempted, must all have been relevant factors (see Hadley *et al.*, 1987).

However, the evidence from this study supports the view that it would be easier to implement policies which call for a switch of emphasis to locally-based, independent provision through the developmental work of managers on the one hand, and workers freed from caseloads on the other hand. The workers in this second category might well not be professional social workers, in the traditional sense. In Oldweigh, for example, there were two fieldworkers who believed themselves to be practising community social work—the outposted worker in the Focus 230 centre and the Under-Fives Day Care Officer—but neither was a qualified social worker and neither had caseload responsibilities.

In both the areas, some community provision for families had been created. In chapter 4 it was demonstrated that individual social workers had not, and could not have, created new provisions of this type. Successful projects, that lasted more than a year or so, owed their foundation to the support of a number of agencies and influential individuals in the community.

In Newpath, the local authority, in cooperation with other statutory and voluntary agencies, managed to set up a larger number of community-based projects for family support. It succeeded in making provision available to children and their families in 'high-need' areas. All the projects developed and drew in large numbers of volunteers in a way that would not have been possible if the local authority had been direct providers. In this sense, Newpath did provide one model of how a local authority social services department might fulfil a part of its duties towards families and children in need *indirectly*, by supporting community provision. However, the research suggested that a social services department that moves in this direction would also have to rethink the roles of its own staff and be prepared for the necessity of restructuring its own work, to make the most of the new provision.

Differences Between the Areas
The similarity of the population structure in the two areas was reflected in the samples of families referred to the social services departments. The

families were alike in structure, and on measures of need. They had a similar number of informal supporters available to them. However, although they came to the departments with similar problems, their outcomes were somewhat different. In Newpath, as described in chapter 9, parents reported more improvement in family problems and showed more change on a standard measure of emotional distress than they did in Oldweigh.

It is not possible to draw firm conclusions about the reasons for this apparent difference. Although the social services department in Newpath itself provided more help, the parents who received it were not the ones whose problems most improved. Families in Newpath reported more contacts with family support resources—under the control of the social services department and outside it. Contact with these resources, and especially the use of day care of various kinds, was associated with improvement in family problems.

Perhaps there was something about living in Newpath—a sense of energy combined with mutual responsibility—that enhanced people's optimism and led to improved morale there.

The descriptive design of this research did not allow causal relationships to be firmly established. There may have been unmeasured differences between the samples of families in the two areas that accounted for any observed differences in outcome. It is possible that bias may have crept in as the researchers deepened their acquaintance with Newpath and formed their own relationships there. Nevertheless, the results of the research lend support to the hypothesis that parents under stress more easily overcome family problems (without developing chronically depressed mood) when there are many sources of family support available in local communities.

References

Adams, P., Dawson, J. and Loveday, S. (1983). *The Walcot Centre: An Evaluation.* The Childrens Society: London.

Alloway, R. and Bebbington, P. (1987). Buffer theory of social support. *Psychological Medicine* **17**, 91–108.

Association of County Councils. (1986). *Family Policy.* Association of County Councils: London.

Azar, S. T. (1988). Methodological considerations in treatment outcome research in child maltreatment. In *Coping with Family Violence: Research and Policy Perspectives.* (ed. G. T. Hotaling, D. Finkelhor, J. T. Kirkpatrick and M. A. Strauss). Sage Publications: Beverly Hills.

Barclay Report. (1982). *Social Workers: Their Roles and Tasks.* Bedford Square Press: London.

Barrera, M. (1981). Social support in the adjustment of pregnant adolescents: assessment issues. In *Social Networks and Social Support* (ed. B. H. Gottlieb). Sage Publications: Beverly Hills.

Barrera, M. (1985). Informant corroboration of social support network data. *Connections* **8(1)**, 9–13.

Barth, R. P. and Ash, J. R. (1986). Identifying screening and engaging high risk clients in private non-profit child abuse prevention. *Child Abuse & Neglect* **10**, 99–109.

Beazley, M. (1989). From paternalism to participation. In *Working Partnerships: Local Authorities and Community Development* (ed. M. Broady and R. Hedley). Bedford Square Press: London.

Bebbington, A. C. and Quine, L. (1986). Evaluating the malaise inventory. *Social Psychiatry* **22**, 5–7.

Becker, S. and MacPherson, S. (1986). *Poor Clients.* University of Nottingham, Department of Social Administration: Nottingham.

Berridge, D. and Cleaver, H. (1987). *Foster Home Breakdown.* Blackwell: Oxford.

Berrueta-Clement, J. *et al.* (1984). Changed lives: the effects of the Perry Preschool Program on youths through age 19. *Monographs of the High/Scope Educational Research Foundation, No. 8.* High/Scope Press: Ypsilanti.

Birchall, D. (1982). *Family Centres.* National Childrens Bureau: London.

Blythe, B. J. (1983). A critique of outcome evaluation in child abuse evaluation. *Child Welfare* **62**, 325–335.

Broady, M. (1983). *The Statutory Authority and Voluntary Social Welfare.* Unpublished.

Bronfenbrenner, U. (1974). *Is Early Intervention Effective?: A Report on Logitudinal Evaluation of Pre-School Programmes. Volume 2.* Office of Child Development, Department of Health Education and Welfare: Washington.

Burgoyne, J. and Clark, D. (1982). Reconstitued families. In *Families in Britain* (ed. R. N. Rapoport, M. P. Fogarty and R. Rapoport). Routledge: London.

Caplan, G., ed. (1974). *Support Systems and Community Mental Health.* Basic Books: New York.

CCETSW (1989). *Welfare Rights in Social Work Education: Report by a Curriculum Development Group.* CCETSW: London.

Chetwynd, J. (1985). Factors contributing to stress in mothers caring for an intellectually handicapped child. *British Journal of Social Work* **15**, 295–305.

Cohn, A. H. and Daro, D. (1987). Is treatment too late? What ten years of evaluative research tell us. *Child Abuse & Neglect* **11**, 433–442.

Cotterill, A. M. (1988). The geographic distribution of child abuse in an inner-city borough. *Child Abuse & Neglect* **12**, 461–467.

Creighton, S. J. (1985). An epidemiological study of abused children and their families in the UK. *Child Abuse & Neglect* **9**, 441–448.

De'Ath, E. (1985). *Self-help and Family Centres: a current initiative in helping the community.* National Childrens Bureau: London.

Department of Health and Social Security (1977). *A Classification of the English Personal Social Services Authorities.* HMSO: London.

Department of Health and Social Security (1978). *Social Assistance: a review of the supplementary benefits scheme in Great Britain.* DHSS: London.

Department of Health and Social Security (1979). *Relations with Social Services: Report of a Joint Study by the Department's Regional Directorate and Social Work Service of the Relationships between Supplementary Benefits Organisation and Social Services.* DHSS: London.

Department of Health and Social Security (1982). *Child Abuse: a Study of Inquiry Reports 1973–1981.* HMSO: London.

Department of Health and Social Security (1985a). *Children in Care of Local Authorities: England.* DHSS: London.

Department of Health and Social Security (1985b). *Review of Child Care Law: Report to Ministers of an Interdepartmental Working Party.* HMSO: London.

Department of Health and Social Security (1985c). *Social Work Decisions in Child Care: Recent Research Findings and their Implications.* HMSO: London.

Department of Health and Social Security (1986). *Inspection of the Supervision of Social Workers in the Assessment and Monitoring of Cases of Child Abuse.* HMSO: London.

Department of Health. (1989a). *An Introduction to the Children Act.* HMSO: London.

Department of Health. (1989b). *Caring For People: Community Care in the Next Decade and Beyond.* HMSO: London.

Donzelot, J. (1980). *The Policing of Families.* Hutchinson: London.

Eekelaar, J. and Maclean M. (1986). *Maintenance After Divorce.* Oxford University Press: Oxford.

Essen, J. and Wedge, P. (1982). *Continuities in Childhood Disadvantages.* Heinemann: London.

Everitt, B. T. (1980). *Cluster Analysis.* Gower: London.

Fordham, P., Poulton, G. and Randle, L. (1979). *Learning Networks in Adult Education.* Routledge: London.

Garbarino, J. and Gillam, G. (1980). *Understanding Abusive Families.* Lexington: Lexington.

Gibbons, J. and Thorpe, S. (1989). Can voluntary support projects help vulnerable families? The work of Home-Start. *British Journal of Social Work* **19**, 189–202.

Glendinning, C. (1986). *A Single Door: Social Work with the Families of Disabled Children.* Allen & Unwin: London.

Goldberg, E. M. and Warburton, W. (1979). *Ends and Means in Social Work.* Allen & Unwin: London.

Goldberg, E. M. (1987). *Support for Families: Practice, Policy and Research.* Joseph Rowntree Memorial Trust: London.

Goldberg, E. M. and Sinclair, I. (1986). *Family Support Exercise.* National Institute for Social Work: London.

Gottlieb, B. H. (1983). *Social Support Strategies: Guidelines for Mental Health Practice.* Sage Publications: Beverly Hills.

Hadley, R. *et al.* (1987). *A Community Social Worker's Handbook.* Tavistock: London.

Handler, J. (1973). *The Coercive Social Worker: British Lessons for American Social Services.* Rand McNally: Chicago.

Harloe, M. (1975). *Swindon: A Town in Transition.* Heineman: London.

Hasler, J. (1984). *Family Centres: Different Expressions Same Principle.* Childrens Society: London.

Hatch, S. and Hinton, T. (1986). *Self Help in Practice: a Study of Contact-a-Family.* Sheffield Univesity Social Services Monographs: Research in Practice Series: Sheffield.

Hill, M. and Laing, P. (1979). *Social Work and Money.* Allen and Unwin: London.

Holman, B. (1986). Prevention: the Victorian legacy. *British Journal of Social Work* **16**, 1–23.

Holman, B. (1988). *Putting Families First: Prevention and Child Care: A Study of Prevention by Statutory and Voluntary Agencies.* Macmillan: Basingstoke.

House of Commons Social Services Committee. (1984). *Second Report from the Social Services Committee, Session 1983–1984: Children in Care.* Volume 1. HMSO: London.

Ingleby, Viscount (Chairman). (1960). *Report of the Committee on Children and Young Persons.* HMSO: London.

Johnson, W. and L'Esperance, J. (1984). Predicting the recurrence of child abuse. *Social Work Research and Abstracts* **20 (2)**.

Jones, D. N. ed. (1982). *Understanding Child Abuse.* Hodder and Stoughton: London.

Jordan, W. (1974). *Poor Parents.* Routledge & Kegan Paul: London.

Knapp, M., Robertson, E. and Thomason, C. (1988). *Public Money, Voluntary Action: Whose Welfare?* University of Kent: Canterbury.

Lazar, I. and Darlington, R. (1982). *Lasting Effects of Early Education: a report from the Consortium for Longitudinal Studies.* Society for Research in Child Development.

Leissner, A. (1967). *Family Advice Centres.* Longmans: London.

Nicol, A. R. *et al.* (1988). A focused casework approach to the treatment of child abuse: a controlled comparison. *Journal of Child Psychology and Psychiatry* **29**, 703–711.

Nolan, T. and Pless, I. B. (1986). Emotional correlates and consequences of birth defects. *Journal of Pediatrics* **109**, 201–216.

Nolan, T. *et al.* (1987). Controlled trial of social work in childhood chronic illness. *Lancet* **i**, 411–415.

Olds, D. L. *et al.* (1986). Preventing child abuse and neglect: a randomised trial of nurse home visitation. *Pediatrics* **78**, 65–78.

Osborn A. F. and Milbank, J. E. (1987). *The Effects of Early Eduction.* Clarendon Press: Oxford.

Packman, J. (1968). *Child Care: Needs and Numbers.* Allen Unwin: London.

Packman, J. (1981). *The Child's Generation.* Blackwell: Oxford.

Packman, J., Randall, J. and Jacques, N. (1986). *Who Needs Care? Social Work Decisions about Children.* Blackwell: Oxford.

Parker, R. A., ed. (1980). *Caring for Separated Children: Plans, Procedures and Priorities.* Macmillan: London.

Parker, R. A. (1988). Residential Care for Children. In *Residential Care: The Research Reviewed* (ed. A. I. C. Sinclair). HMSO: London.

Phelan, J. (1983). *Family Centres: A Study.* Childrens Society: London.

Pless, I. B. & Satterwhite, B. (1972). Chronic illness in childhood: selection, activities and evaluation of non-professional family counsellors. *Clinical Pediatrics* **11**, 403–409.

Provence, S. and Naylor, A. (1983). *Working with Disadvantaged Parents and their Children.* Yale University Press: New Haven.

Rapoport, R. N., Fogarty, M. P. and Rapoport, R., eds. (1982). *Families in Britain.* Routledge: London.

Reinach, E., ed. (1981). *Research Highlights No. 1. Decision Making in Child Care.* Scottish Academic Press: Edinburgh.

Rescorla, L. *et al.* (1982). The Yale child welfare research program: description and results. In *Daycare: Scientific and Social Policy Issues* (ed. E. Zigler and E. Gordon). Auburn House: Boston.

Rivara, F. P. (1985). Physical abuse in children under two: a study of their outcomes. *Child Abuse & Neglect* **9**, 81–87.

Rutter, M., Tizard, J. and Whitmore, K. (1970). *Education, Health and Behaviour.* Longmans: London.

Seitz, V. *et al.* (1985). Effects of family support intervention: a 10 year follow-up. *Child Development* **56**, 376–391.

Sinclair, I. A. C. and Thomas, D. N. (1983). *Perspectives on Patch.* National Institute for Social Work: London.

Smith, J. E. (1984). Non-accidental injury to children: 1. A review of behavioural interventions. *Behaviour Research and Therapy* **22**, 331–347.

Social Service Inspectorate. (1988). *Family Centres: A Change of Name or a Change of Practice.* Department of Health: London.

Starr, R. E. (1982). *Child Abuse Prediction: Policy Implications.* Ballinger: Cambridge.

Stein, R. E. K. and Jessop, D. J. (1986). Long term mental health effects of a pediatric home care program. (Paper presented at Annual Meeting of the Ambulatory Pediatric Association, Washington).

Stewart, G. and Stewart, T. J. (1986). *Boundary Changes: Social Work and Social Security.* Child Poverty Action Group: London.

Stewart, G. *et al.* (1989). *The Social Fund: A Critical Analysis of its Introduction and First Year in Operation.* Association of County Councils: London.

Trickett, P. *et al.* (1982). A five year follow up of participants in the Yale child welfare research program. In *Daycare: Scientific and Policy Issues.* (ed. E. Zigler and E. Gordon). Auburn House: Boston.

Veiel, H. O. F. (1985). Dimensions of social support: a conceptual framework for research. *Social Psychiatry* **20**, 156–162.

Van der Eyken, W. (1982). *Home-Start: A Four-Year Evaluation.* Home-Start Consultancy: Leicester.

Willmott, P. and Willmott, P. (1982). Children and family diversity. In *Families in Britain* (ed. R. N. Rapoport, M. P. Fogarty and R. Rapoport). Routledge & Kegan Paul: London.

Willmott, P. and Mayne, S. (1983). *Families at the Centre.* Bedford Square Press: London.

Wolfenden Committee. (1978). *The Future of Voluntary Organisations.* Croom Helm: London.

Zigler, E. and Valentine, J., eds. (1978). *Project Head Start: A Legacy of the War on Poverty.* Free Press: New York.

Appendix 1

1. Family Projects Activities Profile

2. Joint Policy Statement on Neighbourhood
    Family Projects

Family Projects Activities Profile

Name: Acorn.

Premises: Rent-free, purpose-adapted rooms in local college. Kitchen, and large play area. Access to college facilities.

Average Weekly Users: 20 children and 12 adults.

Staffing: Acting leader, full time, NNEB, female.
Project worker, part time, NNEB, female.
Project worker, part time, NNEB, female.
Project worker, part time, NNEB, female.
Project worker, part time, Art Degree, female.

Volunteers: None—College students help in group work.

Funders: Joint Finance. Children's Society are employing body.

Activities: The Usual Week   Monthly activities indicated/Activities free unless indicated

Age Range	Activities	Who Runs and Numbers	Location	Function		
				Providing a Service	Adult Education	Participation in Centre Running
Adult	Parent programme	Staff	Centre	Training in parent skills plus programme of outside speakers		
Adult	Home visiting	Staff	Centre	Support for parents out of term time or when problems		
20 months – 3 yrs	Group day programme 2 × week	Staff	Centre	Structured programme to help with areas of develop-mental delay		

Family Projects Activities Profile

Name: Ashgrove Neighbourhood Centre.
                     Offices—kitchen—2 large meeting rooms, nursery room.

Premises: In process of moving from large pratten hut attached to disabled
                     centre to purpose built rooms in the Ashgrove Peoples
                     Centre—converted school. Centre will be adjacent to primary
                     school.

Average
Number of
Users
Weekly: 60 to 70 adults + 40 children.

Staff: Project leader, full time, female, not local resident. Community
                     and youth work qualifications.
                     Centre worker, full time, female, not local resident. Comunity and
                     youth work qualifications.
                     Administrative worker, full time, female, not local resident.
                     Cleaner, female, 10 hours per week, centre user.

Volunteers: 15 including three men, mainly from users.

Funders: Department of Environment (75 per cent). To 1988. County
                     Council (25 per cent).

Activities: The Usual Week

Monthly activities indicated/Activities free unless indicated

Age Range	Activities	Who Runs and Numbers	Location	Function — Providing a Service	Adult Education	Participating in Centre Running
0–5 years	Creches for all groups and meetings	Swindon child carers paid workers 40 children per week	At centre	A free service to give parents 'space to do what they want'		
5–16 years	Holiday play school for 5–11 year olds. Began in 1987 by student	2 to 3 volunteers 15 to 20 children in school holiday	At centre	To provide free child care whilst groups running, 'parent space'		
Adult	Individual counselling	80% of the member of staff's time on this	At centre or at user home	A service for individual centre users usually around relationship problems. A service provided a user demand		
Adult	Mums Group (open coffee a.m.) longest running group, going 6 years + and creche	Users themselves, 1 staff member attends 8 users?	At centre	No real aim except time and space for mums to enjoy themselves		
Adult	Child minders support meetings Going 18 months	For the 3 registered child minders on Pinehurst Self-run with 1 staff support	At centre		Aims to educate about practical child minding issues and encourage more people to register as child minders. Group provides a link with social services department	
						Fund raise for centre

Age Range	Activities	Who Runs and Numbers	Location	Function		
				Providing a Service	Adult Education	Participating in Centre Running
Adult	Tuesday Family Lunch Group and creche	Users and 1 staff. 8 mums, 2 dads and childen	This is the only lunch group. Users provide meal at £1 per family. A Family Day			
Adult	Womens Health Set up student in 1987 and creche	User run and 1 staff if required. 6 users	At centre		Looking at womens health needs, yoga, shiatsu, training	
Adult	Keep Fit Group and creche, c.18 months	Paid Instructor 4 to 6 users 20p per session charge	At centre		Set up on local womens suggestion, an informal class for up to 50 year olds	
Adult	Thrift Shop, coffee bar and creche. Open door	6 volunteers 1 staff will over-see. 30 adults and 16 children	At centre	Providing a service to the community encourages new comers	Opportunity to run a small business	
Adult	Welfare rights Advice point	4 volunteers and 1 staff on rota × 2 weekly 6+ users, open to anyone in Pinehurst	Off centre to ensure confidentiality	Local service seen as vital in area of high poverty		
Adult	Telephone, washing machine, photo-copier, type-writer. Widely used.	Free use to any centre user	At centre	To give access to these facilities which many cannot afford		
Adult	Users Group monthly	15–20 led by Management Committee. Chair and three staff	At centre			To get users feedback on activities and ideas on new developments

Local Social Services use Centre as base for Family Access meetings.   60+ years.   No activities specifically for this age group.

Family Projects Activities Profile

Name: The Herding Centre.

Premises: Ex-school classroom—kitchen offices—large meeting room. In junior school grounds.

Average
Weekly
Users: 55–70 adults plus children.

Staffing: Project co-ordinator full time. CSS qualification. Local estate resident. Female employed four years. Family Project worker part time—female—24 hours—local estate resident. PPA course and work experience. Welfare Rights worker part time, female, 12 hours. Has done welfare rights course. Not local resident. Project support worker, female, 20 hours. Local resident. Clerical qualifications. Two domestic assistants, female. Local residents. Job share six hours each.

Volunteers: 28, mainly from users.

Funders: Children's Society (Withdrawing Funding), County Council.

Activities: The Usual Week

Monthly activities indicated/Activities free unless indicated

Age Range	Activities	Who Runs and Numbers	Location	Function		
				Providing a Service	Adult Education	Participating in Centre Running
0–5 years	Time for tots. Activity group began April '88	Run by parents, instigated by staff. 7–8 parents and 10 children.	At centre		Aims are to get parents and children enjoying play	and management
0–5 years	Creches	Staff and volunteers	At centre	To enable adults to participate in groups		
Teenage	Individual counselling for parents with teenagers. Began Jan. 1988	Staff	Off centre	Counselling over teenage problems		
Adult	Family link restarted Jan. '88	Staff with voluteer help (4 volunteers) 3 families being visited	Off centre	Befriending and support mainly to parents with young families but not just the under fives		
Adult	Family link volunteers group and creche	Staff (13 volunteers in group)	Centre		Training and support for volunteers who may go on to help with the family link	
Adult	Creche training	Staff	At centre		Training for volunteers	
Adult	Creche social evening For creche volunteers	Staff (21 attending)	Centre		To discuss serious child care problem plus silly evening for fun	

	Activity	Staffing / Users	Location	Aim	
Adult	Individual support and counselling for personal problems	Staff	At centre	Seen as an essential service to community. Take referrals	
Adult	Coffee morning no creche—there has always been one of these	2 volunteers 25–32 adults and children	Centre	Open to anyone to provide a meeting point for people seeking a friendly place	
Adult	Welfare rights advice	Staff 3–5 users a week	Centre	To provide easily accessible advice in area	
Adult	Discussion group 'no creche' going over 2½ years	User/volunteers 7 mothers and 12 children	Centre		Stable group of mothers discussing anything
Adult	Adult literacy and creche caring for over two years	LEA Adult Education Staff 4 to 12 participants. Staff instigated	Centre		To provide local service with someone to have the children
Adult	Thrift shop began Dec. 1986 and creche for volunteers children	6 volunteers 5–10 customers	At centre	To provide good second hand clothes locally in area of high social need	Opportunity to run small business
Adult	Time Out for Women. Going for a few months. Evening group	1 staff and borough Community Development Neighbourhood Worker (Female) Average 15 users	At centre	A social evening for women of all ages away from the family	
Adult	Moan, groan and compliments session once a month evening	1 staff as facilitator All staff attend plus user/volunteers. Average 15–20 users	At centre		User feedback on all aspects of project and their own inter relationships

Activities: The Usual Week (*continued*)

Age Range	Activities	Who Runs and Numbers	Location	Function		
				Providing a Service	Adult Education	Participating in Centre Running
Adult	General advice and information	All staff involved, open to anyone	At centre	Information service to the community		

The Centre is used by other groups for meetings. These are: (1) The Cubs; (2) Community Centre Committee; and (3) The Tenants Association.

60 years+. No activities aimed specifically at this age group.

Family Projects Activities Profile

Name: Hilldon Neighbourhood Project.

Premises: Pratten Hut, ex school classroom on main estate with offices and one large meeting room—no separate kitchen.
Also uses—Valley Social Centre—wooden hut with large room, kitchen and office.

Average Weekly Users: Probably 50 to 60 plus children.

Staffing: Neighbourhood worker, female, full time. Youth and community work qualification. Not local resident.

Administrative: Assistant, female, full time. Not local resident.
Cleaner, part time. Local resident.

Volunteers: 12—about half are centre users.

Funders: Borough Council (25 per cent). Department of Environment: Urban Aid (75 per cent). To 1989.

Activities: The Usual Week

Monthly activities indicated/Activities free unless indicated

Age Range	Activities	Who Runs and Numbers	Location	Function		
				Providing a Service	Adult Education	Participating in Centre Running
0–5 years	Tiny Tots playtime started late 1986	Started by 1 local resident 11 mothers and 15 children	At Penhill Centre	A chance to meet other mothers and the children to play		
5–6 years	Girls group 12–13 year old started late 1986	2 paid staff, 1 employed by the project, 1 employed by the youth service Used by 12 girls	At Penhill centre	Recognising a need for girls to have own youth club		
Adult	Individual casework with callers and group users	Both staff involved each day Averages 4 people weekly needing support	At Penhill centre	Individual support needed in this area especially problems around marital/family relationship problems		
Adult	General advice and information	Both staff	At Penhill centre	Open door information service on services in the area		
Adult	Use of photocopier and telephone. Try to charge for these	Open access Fairly widely used	At centre	Providing needed facility		
Adult	Welfare Rights Advice Point for anyone in Penhill twice weekly	6 volunteers and 1 staff 11 users on average	At both centres	Local service as there are a lot of claimants in the area		
Adult	Housing Advice Point for Penhill tenants started Oct. 1987	Housing Assistant and 1 volunteer to make coffee 6–10 users	At Valley centre	Local council tenants wanting local contact with Housing Department		

Adult	WOMEN (Women On Mondays: Evading Noise) for mothers with under five year olds	User run but 1 staff to support 5 adults and children use it	Valley centre	Originally aimed at isolated young single parents in the valley—wanted a referral group and group with outside speakers
Adult	Valley centre morning open to anyone	User run with staff support 5 adults and children usually there	Valley centre	Similar to Mothers and Toddlers Group offering somewhere for people to meet socially. Begun by staff member
Adult	Gingerbread coffee morning	Gingerbread paid worker 3 lone parents and children	Penhill centre	Gingerbread saw lots of isolated lone parents in this area. A chance to get together
Adult	Ladies night run for three years monthly evenings	User committee run. 15–20 users	Penhill centre	Started by local resident to give women a friendly secure meeting place—away from pubs

60+. No specific activities for this group.

Other groups use centre. A Gardening Club and the Community Council. They hire the meeting room. Health visitors run a Baby Clinic at the Centre.

Family Projects Activities Profile

Name:			Home-Start.

Premises:		Rented rooms in Trust-owned, central property in poor repair.
				Rented church hall for group activities.

**Average
Weekly
Users:**			80 adults and children.

Staffing:		Organiser part time. CQSW. Assistant Organiser part time. Qualified
				teacher. Secretary part time. Book-keeper, fee for service.

Volunteers:		47 trained. 11 in training.

Activities: The Usual Week

Monthly activities indicated/Activities free unless indicated.

Age Range	Activities	Who Runs and Numbers	Location	Function		
				Providing a Service	Adult Education	Participating in Centre Running
0–5 years	Home visiting	Volunteers supervised by organiser	Home	Friendship and support		
0–5 years	Family group	Organisers volunteers and playgroup volunteers	Church hall	Developing confidence. Stimulation for children. Reducing isolation		
Adult	Training/Support Group	Organisers for volunteers (monthly)	At centre		Training and supervision	
Adult	Induction and training	Organisers for new volunteers weekly at intervals	At centre		Training	

Family Projects Activities Profile

Name: The Meadow Project.

Premises: Staff office and meeting place in rented Borough Council flat, leased for 1 year. Three rooms and a kitchen.
Education Department has promised them ex-classroom Pratten Hut on special school site if they can get £20,000 to move it.

Staff: Family Project worker, full time, female. Began June 1 1988—not local resident. Administrative worker—to be appointed.

Funders: NSPCC.
Social Services.

Activities: Project not begun at time of research. It is intended to base the work and self-help groups in the county and/or at the centre, based on the Scope model. The aim is to devolve responsibility for the groups to their members.

Family Projects Activities Profile

Name: Newton Family Project.

Premises: Four Bedroomed house on mixed council and private housing estate. Kitchen—through lounge as main meeting room. Three offices and meeting room upstairs. Small garden for children's play.

Numbers Using Project Per Week: 55 Adults and children.

Staff: Senior Project worker, male, full-time. HND Management Studies. Certificate in Child Care and Education of Young Persons. Post Qualifying Course in residential care. Not local resident. Project worker, female, full-time, not local resident. Administrative worker, female, part-time.

Volunteers: 33 with 20 active all female, recruited mainly from users.

Funders: National Children's Home.
County Council.

Activities: The Usual Week

Monthly activities indicated/Activities free unless indicated

Age Range	Activities	Who Runs and Numbers	Location	Function		
				Providing a Service	Adult Education	Participating in Centre Running
0–5 years	Creches	Volunteers	At house	Structured safe play whilst parents have a break		
5–16 years	Day trips in holidays	Staff and volunteers	Local parks	Structured breaks in holidays		
Adult	Individual counselling on demand	2 staff average of 4 people each at any 1 time	House or person's home	Give service as not readily available elsewhere. Aware long waiting lists for Relate and child guidance.		
Adult	Befriending service, began 1985	2 staff and a few volunteers. 23 families listed	At user's homes	Mainly referrals from social services and health visitors. Service for young families experiencing difficulties and isolation		
Adult	Welfare Rights Advice Point. Began 1982. Now ×3 per week	5 volunteers 0–8 users per session— open to anyone	At house	Service because of great demand for benefits advice		

Activities: The Usual Week (*continued*)

Age Range	Activities	Who Runs and Numbers	Location	Function		
				Providing a Service	Adult Education	Participating in Centre Running
Adult	Newcomers Group and creche, started in 1986 by volunteers	Groups runs itself with 2–3 creche volunteers. 5–15 adults and children	At house	Volunteers and staff felt the main coffee morning was too noisy to introduce newcomers. A group to gain confidence in the project		
Adult	Coffee morning and creche. Going since 1985. Open door for anyone	2 staff and volunteers, 15–25 adults and children	At house	A social meeting place—a place to make friends		
Adults	Break-aways and creche. Going since 1986. Instigated by staff	1 staff, volunteers and users 8–15 adults and children	At house			Project users wanted a more active group where they could make decisions about activities in the group project
Adult	Toothill Group started 1986	2 MSC workers leaving May '88 3–8 adults and children	Church hall	A referrals group for isolated people, some had been treated at psychiatric hospital. Health visitors asked for group		

Activities: The Usual Week (*continued*)

Age Range	Activities	Who Runs and Numbers	Location	Function		
				Providing a Service	Adult Education	Participating in Centre Running
Adult	Shaw Coffee Morning. Open door. Drop in began 1986	2 MSC staff and group members 6–12 adults and children	Local Community Centre	Social group began by MSC workers when health visitors said area lacked meeting place for young mothers		
Adult and Children	Annual Holiday. Began in 1985	1 staff and group of volunteers 120 parents and children including 15 fathers	Cornwall	Subsidised holiday for families who would not get one normally. Started because people said they wanted this service		
Adult	Fund Raising Committee meets monthly	1 staff and 10 users	At house			Fund raising for the project especially holiday

Over 60 + years. The project has no activities speciafically aimed at this age group.

The Local Social Services use the rooms for family access meetings.

Statement
Neighbourhood Family Projects

This was agreed as a joint statement by representatives of Funders, Workers and Members of Local Management Committees in April 1987.

1.   The development of Neighbourhood Family Projects as joint ventures involving statutory and voluntary agencies, is based upon the following expectations:

   a) They are neighbourhood based—they are often better placed than statutory agencies to know about an area and suitable places for information sharing within their communities.

   b) In promoting health and well being within their communities they have an enabling role to play. They are well placed to develop more informal support and can work in ways which help to avoid people feeling stigmatised when seeking help or advice.

   c) They can *identify and develop new needs.* They are in the position to recognise emerging local needs and unmet existing ones, they can develop the resources for meeting these needs from Statutory and/or voluntary sources.

2.   Each Neighbourhood Family Project will work towards establishing a local Management or Advisory Group which reflects local circumstances. These groups be they management or advisory, will establish objectives and determine priorities. Representatives of funding agencies will be invited to serve on these bodies.

3.   Neighbourhood Family Projects are independent voluntary agencies which are not substitutes for statutory provision. It is essential that their independence is recognised and respected.
        The partnership between projects and statutory agencies requires a close collaboration and commitment on both sides to establish close and relevant working relationships.
        Neighbourhood Family Projects will occasionally experience problems when the expectations of statutory agencies seem to conflict with a project's loyalty towards a family. The statutory agencies accept the importance of a project standing by a family when the project considers this appropriate. It will be important for the relative roles of the projects and the statutory agencies to be clearly understood by each even if differences cannot be resolved.

4.   Recognition and value is given to both the breadth and integrated nature of the work which Neighbourhood Family Projects undertake. It is however recognised that particular funding agencies may find themselves unable to resource all aspects of work.

Workloads and priorities will have to be agreed with the Funding Agencies and will have to take account of the limits imposed by the charitable status of voluntary organisations involved.

NB.—Statutory Agencies refer to Social Services, Health Authority, Education Department, Borough Council, etc.

5. Local Management or Advisory Groups will set up a means of professional support and supervision for their workers which is acceptable to the funders.

6. The funding of Neighbourhood Family Projects is proceeding on the basis of a joint statutory and voluntary commitment (subject to joint negotiation and review). All the funding agencies recognise the legitimacy of the projects' hopes that funding should be planned on a continuing basis.

15th May 1987

This statement was adopted by representatives of:

Ashgrove Neighbourhood Centre and workers.

Newton Centre Management Committee.

Herding Centre Management Committee and workers.

Hilldon Family Centre Management Committee and workers.

Meadow Centre Advisory Group and workers.

N.C.H.

Children's Society.

B County Social Services.

B Health Authority.

B Education Department.

Appendix 2

Statistical Consultation

Appendix 2 summarises a number of statistical reports received from Professor B. S. Everitt (Research and Data Consultants, Sigma X Ltd.).

The **Family Problem Questionnaire** was developed during the pilot stage of the project. Its purpose was to gather information, as simply as possible, about current, perceived family problems. It was designed to be answered by a parent with current day-to-day responsibility for the child(ren). The 39 items were draw from previous research studies of young families and from interviews and observations during pilot stage and were intended to cover the most frequently encountered problems.

The items are in the form of statements to which the respondent is asked to express agreement or disagreement on a five point scale, which is subsequently scored from five for 'strongly agree' to one for 'strongly disagree'. The original questionnaire is reproduced as Table A1.

Development of Scales
The data from baseline interviews with referred parents were submitted to Professor B. S. Everitt for statistical analysis. He advised that analysis was worthwhile only for the combined data set (*ie* from both research areas) due to the comparatively large number of items (39) and small number of cases. There were 138 cases with complete data in the combined sample. The type of analysis used was simple principal components with varimax rotation of the factors. Tables A2 and A3 summarise the results using two samples: all cases from both areas; and cohabiting parents only from both areas.

In Table A2, the first factor might be identified with lack of social contact; the second with parent-child relationships (parenting); the third with financial worries; the fourth is a somewhat puzzling dimension apparently concerned with having a delinquent child and parental attitudes to the child in question; and the fifth represents health problems. In Table A3 (using data from cohabiting cases only) an additional factor—the third—clearly represents marital problems. Mr Everitt advised that a factor model is appropriate and that it would be unwise to summarise the data in a single problem score. A better approach would be to describe each case in terms of scores on scales representing the factors outlined above.

There were nine items which did not load on any of the factors—questions 1, 3, 4, 9, 19, 23, 32, 33, 34. Most of these questions had posed problems in use because of their wording. It was decided to drop them from the analysis and from any subsequent use of the questionnaire in field studies.

Four factors were then related to a number of other variables collected in the community and referral samples. In addition the results of a factor analysis of the Malaise Inventory are briefly described.

Factor analysis of the Malaise Inventory
The Malaise Inventory consists of 24 questions about health coded 1 for having a particular problem and 0 for not have the problem. Amongst the community sample, 353 respondents had complete data. A principle components analysis of the correlations between the 24 items identified 10 components with eigenvalues greater than unity. The first of these was a general health item on which all items

loaded positively; this component accounted for 14 per cent of the total variation in the items, twice as much as the second component. Rotation of the 10 components with eigenvalues greater than unity led to new components which only involved two or three items with substantial loadings. The choice was thus one of producing scores on each of these to relate to the previously derived factors or of simply summing the 24 items to produce a malaise index. For the purpose of this investigation the latter seemed a more sensible proposal.

Relating factor scores from the family problems inventory to other variables
The four most stable factors identified from the Family Problem Questionnaire were: Finance; Social Contact; Health; Marital. Scores on these were used in an analysis of the relationship with other variables. Each factor score was derived simply by averaging appropriate item values.

Although many of the correlations were statistically significant, the only substantial ones involved the Social Disadvantage Index and the Malaise Inventory. The Finance scale was positively correlated with the Social Disadvantage index in both the referral and the community samples. All four scales were positively correlated with the Malaise Inventory in both samples.

Cluster Analysis

The need to classify objects or people is fundamental both for everyday living and, more specifically, in the development of many areas of science. In its most general sense classification is the process of giving names to collections of things which are thought to be similar to each other in some respect. Cluster analysis is a generic term for a large number of techniques designed to construct a classification of a set of objects given a description of each object in terms of a number of numeric variables. Many of these methods have appeared during the last two decades or so, their development approximately paralleling that of the computer on which they depend to undertake the large amount of arithmetic often involved. Reviews and descriptions of the methods are available in Everitt (1980).

Essentially clustering techniques should be considered as useful for the 'exploration' of complex multivariate data. The groups or clusters found may provide a useful summary of the data and may additionally be suggestive of interesting hypotheses which may be tested in future studies. In clustering the referral and community sample data the main aim was to identify groups of people most in need of social services support.

Despite a number of empirical studies no evidence has been produced that suggests that one method of cluster analysis is the most useful in all situations. There is however some evidence which points to a small sub-set of the techniques as being better than others in a variety of circumstances. From this sub-set a 'k-means' algorithm was selected for the analysis. The results of applying the k-means clustering algorithm to both the community and referral samples are described. For each sample, two analyses were performed.

(a) *Using the following variables*

1   Age of main carer

2   Disadvantage index

3   Malaise score

4   Finance

5   Social contact

6   Health

7   Marital

8   Parenting

(b) *Separate analyses of single parents and married couples using again the above eight variables*

Solutions for 2, 3 and 4 groups were reported. Means for the 3-group solution are illustrated in Table A4.

Table A1
Family Problem Questionnaire
Next I'd like to go over with you a list of problems that people with families often have.

GIVE INFORMANT SPECIMEN LIST

Each problem or statement is listed as if it applied to you or your family—For example, 'I would like more help with babysitting'. I would like you to say how much you agree with that statement. In other words, how much does that statement actually fit with your own opinion at the moment. If you agree very much with the statement, as it applies to you and your family, you put a circle round the figure 2 (strongly agree). If you agree at all with the statement, put the circle round 1. If you can't decide one way or the other put a circle round 0. If you disagree at all with the statement, circle -1 and if you disagree very much, circle -2. Would you like me to read out each statement and record your answer, or would you rather read them and mark the answers yourself?

Please ask any questions you like as we go along to make it clearer.

> 2 Strongly agree
> 1 Agree
> 0 Uncertain
> -1 Disagree
> -2 Strongly disagree

1 Our family has had to cope with a big change recently   2   1   0   −1   −2

2 I often feel lonely   2   1   0   −1   −2

3 I lost someone important to me recently   2   1   0   −1   −2

4 I would like some help in coping with big changes in my   2   1   0   −1   −2
life

5 I would like to go out socially more often   2   1   0   −1   −2

6 My husband/wife/partner and I seem to have a lot of   2   1   0   −1   −2
rows

7 I would like some help in getting along better with   2   1   0   −1   −2
someone important to me

8 My husband/wife/partner and I seem to find it difficult   2   1   0   −1   −2
to talk to each other about important things

9 I find it difficult to do domestic jobs like cooking and   2   1   0   −1   −2
cleaning as well as I would like

10 Our family is facing a lot of problems at the moment   2   1   0   −1   −2

11 I feel I/we need some help with the job of being parents   2   1   0   −1   −2

12 I find control and discipline of the children is a problem   2   1   0   −1   −2

13 It is difficult to find enjoyable things to do with the   2   1   0   −1   −2
children

14 My husband/wife/partner and I can talk to each other   2   1   0   −1   −2
about things that might be upsetting us

15 I feel I have a satisfying social life   2   1   0   −1   −2

16 I am really worried about one or more of the children   2   1   0   −1   −2

17 I don't feel as affectionate as I would like towards one   2   1   0   −1   −2
or more of the children

18 I feel pretty confident as a mother/father   2   1   0   −1   −2

19 I/We need advice about how to get welfare benefits   2   1   0   −1   −2
we are entitled to

20 We are having difficulties getting what we need from   2   1   0   −1   −2
an organisation (like DHSS or social services)

21 Our family really needs some help at the moment   2 1 0 −1 −2

22 We are in difficulties because one of the family is in 2 1 0 −1 −2
trouble with the law

23 I don't have any real difficulty in contacting organ- 2 1 0 −1 −2
isations like social security, social services, or schools
to ask for what I want

24 At the moment one of my main problems is feeling 2 1 0 −1 −2
upset or depressed

25 Illness in the family is a problem at the moment   2 1 0 −1 −2

26 I would describe my health as poor   2 1 0 −1 −2

27 I would like more help with my health problems   2 1 0 −1 −2

28 Our family has quite a few money worries   2 1 0 −1 −2

29 I am worried about debts or rent arrears   2 1 0 −1 −2

30 I would say our family has quite a few money worries 2 1 0 −1 −2

31 We need practical help with our financial problems   2 1 0 −1 −2

32 I need more practical help in the house   2 1 0 −1 −2

33 I sometimes need help with finding somewhere for one 2 1 0 −1 −2
or more of the children to go during the day (e.g.
playgroup, nursery, childminder)

34 On the whole, our family is doing pretty well at the 2 1 0 −1 −2
moment

35 I would like more help with babysitting or care for the 2 1 0 −1 −2
children after school

36 I feel I sometimes need a complete break from the 2 1 0 −1 −2
children for a short while

37 I find it difficult or expensive to get to the shops, 2 1 0 −1 −2
doctor, etc.

38 I am sometimes worried about my wife/husband/ 2 1 0 −1 −2
partner's violence

39 I sometimes worry that I will lose control and harm 2 1 0 −1 −2
one of the children

Table A2
Family Problem Questionnaire: Analysis of combined data: 35 questions: 138 cases

Variables with Rotated Factor Loadings Greater than 0.5

Factor 1	Factor 2	Factor 3	Factor 4	Factor 5
2	7	20	17	25
5	11	28	18	26
15	12	29	22	27
35	13	30		
37	16	31		
	36			

% Variance Accounted for:

10.8	10.3	10.3	6.8	6.8

The first 5 factors account for 45 per cent of the variance

Table A3
Family Problem Questionnaire: Analysis of combined data for 60 cohabiting cases

Variables with Rotated Factor Loadings Greater than 0.5

Factor 1	Factor 2	Factor 3	Factor 4	Factor 5
2	20	6	25	3
7	28	8	26	9
10	29	14	27	
11	30	22		
12	31	38		
13				
16				
21				
24				

% Variance Accounted for:

13.8	12.6	7.9	7.7	7.2

The first 5 factors account for 49.2 per cent of the variance

Table A4
Grouping of Referred Families According to Needs

Groups	Age	Disad. Index	Finance	Health	Parent/ Child	Social Contact	Marital	Malaise
				Couples: Mean Scores				
1 (n=17)	31.7	6.4	3.9	3.3	3.5	4.2	3.2	11.8
2 (n=25)	26.2	7.4	4.1	1.8	2.1	3.5	2.4	6.5
3 (n=29)	31.7	5.5	2.8	2.0	2.0	2.4	2.0	4.5
				Lone Parents: Mean Score				
1 (n=21)	30.9	7.7	4.3	3.8	3.3	4.2		15.8
2 (n=28)	25.9	7.4	4.0	1.5	2.4	4.2		8.9
3 (n=22)	35.2	6.8	2.9	1.9	2.2	2.6		5.6

Table A5
Grouping of Community Families

Groups	Age	Disad. Index	Finance	Health	Parent/ Child	Social Contact	Marital	Malaise
				Couples: Mean Score				
1 (n=89)	31.9	1.5	2.6	1.9	2.1	3.0	2.0	8.4
2 (n=220)	31.4	0.8	1.3	1.1	1.5	2.1	1.2	2.7
				Lone Parents: Mean Score				
1 (n=17)	29.8	2.3	3.4	1.7	2.4	3.5		9.0
2 (n=30)	32.8	1.4	1.8	1.3	1.5	2.4		3.5

Missing data on 3 cases

Printed in the United Kingdom for HMSO
Dd 292856   C15   9/90